MANAGING EMPLOYEES WITHOUT FEAR

MANAGING EMPLOYEES WITHOUT FEAR

How to Follow the Law, Build a Positive Work Culture, and Avoid Getting Sued

Adam Rosenthal

Society for Human Resource Management
Alexandria, Virginia I shrm.org

Society for Human Resource Management, India Office
Mumbai, India I shrmindia.org

Society for Human Resource Management
Haidian District Beijing, China I shrm.org/cn

Society for Human Resource Management, Middle East and Africa Office
Dubai, UAE I shrm.org/pages/mena.aspx

SHRM®
BETTER WORKPLACES
BETTER WORLD™

This publication is designed to provide accurate and authoritative information regarding the subject matter covered. It is sold with the understanding that neither the publisher nor the author is engaged in rendering legal or other professional service. If legal advice or other expert assistance is required, the services of a competent, licensed professional should be sought. The federal and state laws discussed in this book are subject to frequent revision and interpretation by amendments or judicial revisions that may significantly affect employer or employee rights and obligations. Readers are encouraged to seek legal counsel regarding specific policies and practices in their organizations.

This book is published by the Society for Human Resource Management (SHRM). The interpretations, conclusions, and recommendations in this book are those of the author and do not necessarily represent those of the publisher.

SHRM books and products are available on most online bookstores and through the SHRMStore at www.shrmstore.org.

SHRM creates better workplaces where employers and employees thrive together. As the voice of all things work, workers and the workplace, SHRM is the foremost expert, convener and thought leader on issues impacting today's evolving workplaces. With 300,000+ HR and business executive members in 165 countries, SHRM impacts the lives of more than 115 million workers and families globally. Learn more at SHRM.org and on Twitter @SHRM.

Library of Congress Cataloging-in-Publication Data
Names: Rosenthal, Adam R., author.
Title: Managing employees without fear : how to follow the law, build a positive work
   culture, and avoid getting sued / Adam Rosenthal.
Description: First edition. | Alexandria: Society for Human Resource Management, 2021.
   | Includes bibliographical references and index. |
Identifiers: LCCN 2020054923 (print) | LCCN 2020054924 (ebook) | ISBN
   9781586446642 (paperback) | ISBN 9781586646653 (pdf) | ISBN 9781586446666
   (epub) | ISBN 9781586446673 (mobi)
Subjects: LCSH: Labor laws and legislation—United States. | Personnel management.
Classification: LCC KF3319 . R67 2021 (print) | LCC KF3319 (ebook) | DDC
   344.730102/4658—dc23
LC record available at https://lccn.loc.gov/2020054923
LC ebook record available at https://lccn.loc.gov/2020054924

Printed in the United States of America

FIRST EDITION

PB Publishing 10 9 8 7 6 5 4 3 2 1   61.15201

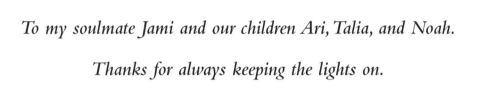

To my soulmate Jami and our children Ari, Talia, and Noah.

Thanks for always keeping the lights on.

Table of Contents

Foreword

How often managers and human resources practitioners flock to legal updates! True, our laws change frequently in light of the constant twists and torques in case law interpretations and in response to changes in technology as well as social movements. But the real appeal of annual or midyear legal updates lies in garnering uninterrupted time with senior employment defense litigation partners at major law firms. After all, these are the gods of the employment law world who can help our organizations when we need them most: when we're threatened with litigation, especially the kind that carries with it the potential for punitive damages. What are they seeing from their mountaintops as far as upcoming trends? Which recent twists in the law should corporate leaders focus on as "game changers" that could otherwise derail the successful trajectory of their organizations? Most important, what golden nuggets of advice and wisdom can they share with their audience, not only in terms of insulating companies from liability but also in terms of catapulting them to becoming *employers of choice* based on their best practices and leadership wisdom?

In fact, wouldn't it be a step better to spend hours of one-on-one time with a leading employment attorney from a major law firm to "skill up" your entire leadership team, not only on the basics of employment law but on the newest facets of recent interpretations and practical guidance that reflect real-life realities and examples? Well, look no further. You've got that ability in your hands as we speak. Developed over decades of employment guidance to companies large and small, for- and non-profit, service and manufacturing, union and nonunion, Adam Rosenthal's *Managing Employees Without Fear* highlights the history, background, lessons, and real-life employment scenarios that build core muscle in the critical areas of leadership offense and leadership defense. Whether you're looking to strengthen your hiring and onboarding practices, enhance your team's practical awareness of wrongful termination and discrimination challenges, or proactively develop your organization's diversity, equity, and inclusion practices, *Managing Employees Without Fear* will provide you with laser-focused issues, real-life scenarios, and legal and ethical solutions that provide your organization with opportunities to flex and pivot rather than lock down in fear.

The author even lets us in on a little secret. This book's title was originally imagined as *Employment Law Confidential*—a behind-the-scenes look at HR and leadership perspectives from the eyes of a seasoned employment attorney. How do operational managers and HR practitioners differ from employment attorneys in their views of workplace matters like performance reviews, progressive discipline, or the potential for allegations that could lead to harassment and discrimination claims? Why is it that a sharp set of legal eyes has a way of cutting through decision-making clutter so efficiently, and wouldn't it be great if we could build that muscle in our own team and in ourselves? How much would a company benefit from enlightened leaders who appreciate the importance of the soft skills that drive employee engagement and retention, trust, and respect? Even more, wouldn't we all want to be part of a company that looks to ethical and moral practices above and beyond what's required by law?

There's so much wisdom in these pages, created by a senior attorney at a major law firm who's willing to share his experiences, tips, and guidelines with you as the reader. *Managing Employees Without Fear* will go a long way in raising your awareness of the importance of the written record; how particular documentation might look in the eyes of a judge, arbitrator, jury member, or even—yes—plaintiff's attorney; and how your actions could be challenged under the microscope of legal scrutiny. But fear not: the whole purpose of this book is to increase your confidence, raise your awareness, and strengthen your organization's ability to put its best foot forward in all leadership practices—both offensive and defensive in nature.

But wait, there's more! Wage and hour class action lawsuits, leading remote teams, dealing with microaggressions in the workplace, social media caveats, data security and privacy matters, and adjusting for implicit bias are all on the agenda and up for discussion. *Managing Employees Without Fear* addresses today's critical topics while enveloping them in a halo of ethics and morals that help you make the right decision—not just the most legally defensible one—every time.

Congratulations in choosing such a successful employment litigation partner in Adam Rosenthal as your career guide and mentor. Rely on his advice, listen to his words closely, and garner in hours the wisdom that took him decades to cultivate. Your investment in this book will be well rewarded, whether you're an HR practitioner, frontline operational leader, or seasoned executive. This is the type of book that builds leadership muscle and success-ful careers. *Managing Employees Without Fear* will help you strengthen your leadership confidence and pass along wisdom of your own as you grow and develop in your own career and pay it forward to the generations that are to follow you.

—Paul Falcone

HR Executive and Bestselling Author of *101 Tough Conversations to Have with Employees* and *101 Sample Write-Ups for Documenting Employee Performance Problems*

CHAPTER 1

What Type of Manager Are You?

"Being a manager is hard enough without having to actually manage people," said a client lamenting that she had been named in an employment lawsuit for telling a new hire he could not bring his 65-pound Belgian Sheepdog—his "support animal"—to the restaurant where he was just hired as a server.

Having spent my entire professional life defending managers and companies in employment lawsuits, I have found that most leaders are surprised and often frightened when they learn that a former employee is claiming they were mistreated at work and is demanding a king's ransom to avoid a lawsuit. While most leaders have heard of *others* in their position who have been entangled in lawsuits by former employees, they never thought it would happen to them. The mystery, of course, is not why are we experiencing an epidemic of employment lawsuits—which I will unpack in the next chapter—but why are so many leaders ill-prepared to prevent these lawsuits from happening in the first place?

The answer to this question is remarkably simple. Far too many companies either do little to train their managers on how they can avoid employment lawsuits or, worse, naively believe their leaders will learn these essential lessons by osmosis. In the midst of this crisis in the American workforce, we are miles past the exit sign for being discreet about how to deal with this serious problem. Employers across the country need to open their eyes and recognize that rather than spending hundreds of millions of dollars every year defending themselves against these lawsuits, they need to fix the root problem by developing leaders who are able to manage without fear.

If you are reading this book, it either means your employer takes employment law compliance issues very seriously and required you to read it, or you are taking it upon yourself to become better educated in this arena. Either way, after reading this book you will be significantly ahead of your fellow managers when it comes to developing concrete steps to better protect your employees, your company, and (let's be very clear) yourself from being caught in a web of expensive and counterproductive employment disputes.

Managing without fear does not mean disregarding the law because a leader does not fear the consequences of their decision. That is managing without a brain. Rather, managing without fear is knowing that because your employees are being treated fairly in accordance with the law, you can be proud of every personnel decision you make. Managing without fear is simply being able to approach difficult employment situations with the confidence that you are acting within the law and that, if challenged, your decisions will be viewed as appropriate and lawful. It is also managing without a fear of crossing the line or being taken advantage of by employees who try to blame their manager for their own shortcomings.

In learning how to manage without fear, it is important to first recognize that there is not a "one-size-fits-all" approach to managing employees. Anyone who believes in the mythical platonic leader that all other managers should model themselves after has never actually spent time in the trenches managing employees. With that in mind, this book hopes to assist every manager—regardless of style, temperament, and ability—to better understand and internalize how to improve their managerial skills in compliance with the law in every interaction they have with their subordinates.

At this point, you may be a bit skeptical about how this book will make you a stronger manager. I get that. Cynicism is a natural trait of a successful leader. With the understanding that there are many different types of successful managers, this book is intended to speak to every shade of leader and offer a positive return on their investment.

So what type of leader are you? Having represented a variety of leaders over the years, I have discovered that there are five general categories of managers. Conveniently, these five categories correlate with five stereotypical American high school caricatures (a mash-up of characters from *The Breakfast Club* and *Beverly Hills, 90210*). As you read the profiles below, ask yourself: "Which description best fits my managerial style?" How honestly you answer this question will have an impact on how much influence this book ultimately has on improving your managerial style and potential success.

THE STUDENT COUNCIL PRESIDENTS

These managers are the proverbial company superstars. They are effective leaders in their organizations and tend to be beloved by their employees and superiors alike. They are usually extroverts who are exceptionally hardworking and goal-oriented. These individuals either have extensive employment law knowledge (because they are the 1 percent of managers who regularly read the employee handbook cover-to-cover and attend every optional HR seminar) or intuitively tend to make the right decisions even if they have to wing it. When these managers have to make a difficult decision, such as whether or not to terminate an underperforming employee, they are typically spot on in their assessment and supremely confident in their judgment.

THE RESERVED HONOR STUDENTS

The second category includes smart and effective managers who are averse to conflict by nature. These managers are successful yet understated leaders in their organizations. They excel in one-on-one coaching and take great pride when a member of their team displays considerable progress. Their greatest challenge as managers is making difficult employment decisions. Having to complete annual performance reviews for underperforming team members is often an anxiety-inducing experience. When faced with an employee who is a chronic underperformer, they tend to focus on the employee's positive attributes and downplay the employee's "opportunities" (this manager prefers to refer to negative attributes as "opportunities"). This creates a considerable headache for the Human Resources (HR) department, because when this manager ultimately reaches the conclusion that the employee should be disciplined or separated (this manager never "fires" anyone), the string of positive annual reviews do not paint an accurate picture of the employee's poor performance. There are a variety of reasons why this manager has difficulties (excuse me, "opportunities") dealing with conflict. Some never fully grasped, or were never trained to appreciate, the central role they play in attracting and retaining top talent while exiting underperformers. Many others simply like to be liked, and avoid conflict whenever possible. This sometimes makes them easy targets for being taken advantage of by their subordinates. Others simply live in a perpetual state of fear that they will make the wrong decision and be accused of violating company policy—or worse, the law.

THE POPULAR JOCKS

These are the managers who reached the manager rung either because:

1. There was no one else to plug into that role, or
2. Upper management had reason to believe that this "people person," with enough experience and training, could become a successful manager.

These managers typically get along with their subordinates and usually do a decent job of motivating others. While these managers are usually well-intentioned, they often lack the tools to issue spot potential employment law issues. These managers often make employment decisions from the gut, without first consulting with HR or considering the consequences of their decisions. These managers also tend to enjoy their jobs and earnestly want to become better managers, but they often don't know which questions to ask. They get easily overwhelmed when it comes to tricky employment law issues. These are the managers that the writers of the legendary TV series *The Office* conjured up when they created Steve Carell's epic character Michael Scott.

THE CHAMPION DEBATERS

These managers are the classic "top-down" generals. They live by the creed that it is better to be respected than to be liked. These managers tend to be very smart, hardworking, and successful. They lack the "warm and fuzzy" characteristics that most people prefer in their leaders and make up for it with their determination to succeed and have the members of their team succeed with them. Often mistaken for being "bad actors" (legalese for managers who violate the law), these individuals actually tend to pride themselves on being rule followers. These managers expect a lot from their employees because they expect a lot from themselves. For this reason, these managers do not equivocate when they have to discipline an employee for not performing to their expectations. They have no trouble separating work from personal life. For these managers, work is work and home is home and the two shall not intersect. These managers are an easy target for employment lawsuits for two reasons. First, as compared to the previous three manager types, these managers tend to terminate more underperformers because they often do not have the patience or desire to coach or "manage out" employees that are not working out. And as more employees are involuntarily separated, the risk increases for more employment lawsuits. And second, because these managers have sharp elbows, their no-nonsense personalities are misunderstood as a pretext for some unlawful motive when, in reality, they actually tend to make decisions based on entirely objective performance criteria.

THE JERKS

The last, and rarest of breeds, are the bona fide jerks. These employees are on a constant power trip and seem to take pleasure in making their subordinates' lives miserable. While the average mid-career adult has had dozens of managers (the majority of whom fit into one of the first four categories), it is not difficult to summon the horrible memories we have when we think of our worst managers. Unless they own the company or make so much money for the company that all other issues are overlooked, these managers typically do not last long in their managerial roles. The jerks are eventually exited out of the organization because enough people complain about their managerial style or the individuals themselves recognize they will end up unemployed with few job prospects if they can't radically transform their approach to dealing with employees in a work setting.

So which type of manager are you? I have asked this question of hundreds of managers over the years, and most initially respond that they are either the Student Body President or the Champion Debater (not surprisingly, no one admits being a Jerk). However, on further reflection, and after I ask respondents to be brutally honest, most admit that depending on the day or the employee interaction, they have elements of the main four personality types.

I wrote this book with three objectives in mind. First, I believe that companies that invest in training their managers to handle real world employment issues have happier employees, a more productive workforce, and save millions of dollars on preventable employment lawsuits. Second, I have trained thousands of managers on a variety of human resources compliance issues, and I am convinced that no matter the manager personality type, the lessons, stories, and warnings contained in these pages will transform how managers approach their subordinates when faced with challenging employment situations. And finally, I wrote this book because I saw a desperate need for this type of practical real-world advice on HR legal compliance. In surveying the marketplace of existing books, I found that previous efforts have either been hyper-technical and much better suited for an HR professional (or worse, an HR lawyer) rather than a frontline leader, or they have frankly been out of touch with reality. This book offers a different approach. While we cover the important legal issues that every manager needs to be aware of in order to:

1. follow company policy,
2. comply with the law, and
3. avoid lawsuits,

we also stay grounded in the "real world" and provide advice that every manager can immediately incorporate into their daily routine.

For the superstar manager (our Student Body President), this book will hone your skills as a leader, particularly if you have only had limited dealings with truly difficult employees and complicated employment situations. While some of the pointers and best practices in this book are things that you likely already embrace, you will learn new ways to approach complicated situations. If you are truly the luminary you aspire to be, then as your career progresses, you will continue to climb the corporate ladder until such time as you are at or near the top. This means that in the future you will likely be in a position with the tremendous responsibility of managing a team of other managers. When you get to that point, it will become obvious to you that not every manager has the same aptitude that made you a successful leader. Because of this, you will spend a considerable amount of time and energy training other managers. The lessons in this book will help guide you as you train others on how to manage within the law, but without fear, and ultimately protect your employees and the organization from potentially costly missteps. The time you spend reading this book will pay considerable dividends for your future career progression.

For the manager who often has anxiety when dealing with challenging employment situations, this book will give you actual tools you can use in your day-to-day interactions that will make you more confident in your decisions, less scared of slipping up, and more successful in the eyes of your superiors. All too often I see underperforming employees figure out how to game the system by exploiting managers who are seen as weak. In these pages, we examine why this is happening, as well as what proactive steps managers can take to prevent this. We explore the steps from making better hiring decisions to implementing effective progressive discipline procedures. To be clear, being cautious when faced with a difficult employment situation is not only a good thing, but also a necessary component of a highly functioning organization. The purpose of this book is not to displace a company's HR department by deputizing every manager to make independent HR decisions. On the contrary, managers who embrace the lessons of this book will be better prepared to interpret the signals that a potential employment law issue is simmering, and then bring HR into the conversation well before the issue boils over.

For the newer manager who has many questions about how to comply with a variety of employment laws, but is lacking quality answers, this book will provide you with a grand tour (which at times is both scenic and treacherous) of the complicated employment law landscape. For those managers who are required to read this book, I have tried as much as possible not to make it feel like homework, as my objective is to serve as a valuable resource as you embark on your managerial journey.

For the hard-driving, no-nonsense manager who has little patience for employees who are not objectively successful, this book will help you recognize that many costly employment disputes can be avoided when managers show a little more patience and a lot more compassion. While this may come across as being soft and conflicts with the vaunted principles of a meritocracy (where everyone is evaluated on the same objective criteria), the fact is that when it comes to difficult employment issues that end up with a plaintiff and a defendant, the optics of the situation are often just as important (and in some cases even more significant) than the actual evidence. My goal is not to convert tough managers into teddy bears. Instead, by shining a spotlight on common areas of conflict, it is my hope that these managers can better navigate difficult situations. The end goal is to foster a more productive and healthy workforce, which will more often than not save the manager from having to defend their decisions in front of a jury.

And for the "Grade A" jerk, while no one would typically place themselves into this category, let's face it: from time to time we all have our moments, particularly when facing a management crisis. The good news is that if you feel less respected by your subordinates or even your peers, it doesn't take much to change the type of leader you are. This book can help you soften some of the rougher edges to make you a stronger and more secure leader.

I want to share a few final notes before we jump into the jungle of employment law for managers.

To My Manager Readers

As an attorney who spends many hours every day writing for judges, one of the pleasures in writing this book is that I was able to speak directly to non-lawyers in a more laid-back style that fits nicely with my Southern California roots. I have intentionally avoided several of the tenets of traditional legal writing, and in its place, I have tried to infuse a bit of levity and humor. However, because many employment laws are at the core of some of our nation's most important and sacred social and economic values, such as preventing discrimination and harassment in the workplace and paying employees properly, it is important that you do not interpret my relaxed style to mean that these issues are not critically serious. Having sat in far too many employment law presentations that cover all of the bases but put half of the audience to sleep, I firmly believe that this book will have a greater impact on your role as a manager if you actually enjoy reading it. Simply put, I am confident that my readers can walk and chew gum at the same time— discussing serious legal issues while enjoying what they are reading.

On a related note, this book is obviously not intended to replace your organization's employment policies and procedures. This book merely supplements your managerial training. In the unlikely event that any of my recommendations and best practices conflict with your organization's policies or recent changes in the law, you should abide by your employer's policies and those changes. As always, when in doubt, consult with your HR department.

To the HR Professional

Take a deep breath. Encouraging your managers to incorporate the lessons contained in these pages will not put you out of a job. If you mandate that all of your managers read this book (for which I would be forever grateful), you are making a wise decision by engaging in what lawyers like to call "preventative law" and what those in the business world aptly refer to as "common sense." Ensuring that your organization's managers develop an internal radar to spot tricky employment issues, and avoid others, will make your job more fulfilling and will make you a more valuable asset to your organization. The ultimate goal is that frontline leaders will work with HR earlier in the process when they have concerns about a problematic employee or challenging situation, with the hope that you can avoid unnecessary employment disputes and expensive litigation. In fact, the only professionals who should be threatened by this book are potential plaintiffs' employment lawyers, who will have fewer companies to sue. To my fellow employment lawyers, my deepest apologies.

Any book authored by an attorney would not be complete without a warning. Unless you and your organization retain me and my law firm, I am not your lawyer and this book is not intended to provide you legal advice. Employment law is particularly captivating because it is constantly evolving and being reinterpreted, and because every employment law situation presents unique facts, characters, and recommended outcomes. If you bought this book because your company just got sued by an ex-employee and you want to figure out what to do, I suggest you put the book down and consult with an experienced employment attorney. Of course, if you are in that situation (and once you get a handle on what happened and whether the ex-employee's claims have merit), I strongly recommend you pick this book back up and read what you could have possibly done to prevent the lawsuit in the first place.

Lastly, before we begin, I challenge you to be honest with yourselves as you read each chapter. Managing employees successfully and within the stringent boundaries of the law is neither easy nor intuitive. To help get you in the right frame of mind, I suggest that when one of the subjects in this book resonates with your own experience, you ask yourself the following three questions:

1. Have I done something in the past that was potentially problematic or could have been viewed from an outsider's perspective as being improper?
2. Looking back at that situation, are there any concrete things I could have implemented to avoid, or at least mitigate, the issue?
3. In the future, what proactive measures will I take to help prevent that issue from happening again?

CHAPTER 2

How Did We Get Here?

American companies spend hundreds of millions of dollars every year on employment-related litigation. And that represents only the hard, out-of-pocket costs associated with defending, settling, and paying judgments to former employees. It does not take into account the loss of productivity, disruption to business, and impact on morale that are all byproducts of every employment lawsuit. As Americans, we collectively have a problem that is in desperate need of a solution: too many employees are filing too many employment lawsuits often because frontline managers make regrettable and entirely avoidable mistakes. This is a problem that every manager who cares about their employees, the organization they work for, and their own job security must help solve. It is a problem that needs "disrupters" like you. However, before we address how to solve this problem, we must first uncover how we arrived at this point.

How did we get here? And by here, I am specifically referring to the uniquely American litigious employment environment where companies of all shapes and sizes are constantly being bombarded by claims from disgruntled employees. It is important to approach this question from two very different perspectives—the macro and micro levels. At the macro level we will briefly analyze the sweeping historical and economic factors that, with few exceptions, have brought very positive and much-needed changes in the workplace. These include laws governing minimum wage and mandating equal employment, as well as prohibitions against discrimination, harassment, and unlawful retaliation. Next, we will examine the 10 micro factors that are often the catalysts that turn ordinary employees into angry plaintiffs. Appreciating both the macro and micro factors will, in turn, help you do a better job protecting yourself and your employees.

THE MACRO FACTORS

In his book, *The World Is Flat: A Brief History of the Twenty-First Century*, Thomas Friedman describes how a confluence of historical events coupled with the creation of the internet and a paradigm shift in how companies and people buy and sell goods (from global supply chains to outsourcing jobs to foreign technology hubs) has created a "flat world." According to Friedman, this new "flat world" has produced tremendous benefits and many challenges.

The "flattening" of the world, along with the generational shift from baby boomers to millennials, and now Gen-Z, has had an especially significant impact on the relationship between employers and their employees, and in turn the relationship between individual frontline leaders and their subordinates.

There are a variety of factors that social scientists point to as evidence of this rapidly changing dynamic. One often-cited example is the steep decline in union membership over the past 50 years from 35 percent of all workers in 1954 to less than 11 percent today. Only 6.4 percent of private-sector employees are members of unions.[1] As a result, unless you work for the government or are in one of the few industries where unions have survived (which likely means you work in hospitality, healthcare, or construction), you have always been an "at-will" employee (i.e., a "free agent" with the ability to jump from one company to the next without any negative repercussions). Regardless of whether you are politically for or against unions, or are agnostic on the subject, the net impact of this trend has been that employees have less loyalty to their employer and are more willing to jump to another job when the right opportunity presents itself. On the flip side, it also means that employers have the ability to quickly separate "at-will" employees without having to go through exhaustive grievance procedures.

Another example of the flattening effect on the American workforce is the dramatic increase in Americans who are self-employed (up to 30 percent of today's workforce).[2] On a recent visit to San Francisco for a client meeting, I spent an hour talking to my 25-year-old Uber driver about his mission in life, which is to never have a boss tell him what to do and when to do it. That means that in addition to driving for Uber and Lyft, he is completing an online MBA and spends most weekends as a freelance painting instructor and bartender. While these "disruptive" labor models will not completely dismantle the traditional employee-employer relationship, it has been and will continue to be an attractive option for individuals who are not interested in fixed hours, annual performance reviews, and watered-down company coffee. It also means that companies needing employees (that cannot justify having independent contractors) must become more attractive places to work and offer workers opportunities and benefits they would not otherwise receive from the "gig" economy.

There is no question that the flattening of the world, and the social and political movements that have emerged in response to globalization and technological advancements, are having a significant impact on the workforce. The uncertainty spurred by globalization has led, at least from my vantage point, to increased strife in the workplace, which in turn has created a rolling tide of employment litigation. As shown in Table 2.1 on the next page, future historians will likely reference a series of events over the last forty years, many of them especially positive steps in creating a more just and equal society, which have also led, at a macro level, to an uptick in workplace strife.

The significance of these events and trends, independently and combined, cannot be overstated. They have led to angry debates, from the halls of Congress to the office water-cooler, and have largely characterized the polarized composition of the U.S. political map. Depending on your political philosophy and the role you believe government should play in the economy and the workforce, you likely have a strong opinion on a variety of hot button issues that directly impact the employment law landscape. These issues include, for example:

1. Free trade/globalization vs. isolation/tariffs
2. Higher minimum wage vs. free market capitalism

Table 2.1.

Decade	Events
1980s	The power and role of private sector unions continued its steep downward trajectory (which started in earnest in the 1950s), upending many of the mechanisms employees and employers had traditionally used to resolve workplace conflicts, and the relationship between employees and employers.
	Expanded opportunities for women and minorities in the workplace, and the diversification of the private sector.
	Emerging popularity of television shows that regularly address employment law themes (e.g., L.A. Law, followed in later years by Ally McBeal, Boston Legal, etc.).
1990s	Proliferation of "pro-employee" laws and regulations, particularly at the state level, and greater awareness of how these laws can be used by employees to go after "bad actors" in the workplace.
	The televised Supreme Court confirmation hearings of Justice Clarence Thomas, which focused largely on allegations of sexual harassment brought by Anita Hill. For many Americans this was the first public discussion on the epidemic of sexual harassment in the workplace.
	The end of the Cold War.
	Expansion of free trade and the North American Free Trade Act (NAFTA).
	Beginning of the internet age and mass telecommunications, which starting in the 2000s, resulted in the democratization of knowledge and the rise of the "Armchair Lawyer."
	Expansion of attorneys that specialize in employment law, on both the plaintiff/employee side as well as the employer/defense side.
2000s	Graying of the baby boomer generation that has led to greater awareness of age discrimination concerns in the workplace.
	The Great Recession and the fallout from the Occupy Wall Street and Tea Party movements.
	Rise of the millennial workforce and competition from the gig economy.
	Solidification of the red/blue divide and the real or perceived hyper-politicization at the U.S. Supreme Court, particularly on issues involving employment laws and regulations.
2010–2020	The #MeToo movement and the literal and figurative "cleaning house" in government and corporate America of (mostly) men who used their power and position to sexually harass and intimidate their female colleagues.
	The enacting of employment laws by cities, further complicating an already complex employment law landscape.
	COVID-19, mass unemployment, the migration of millions of employees from working in offices to working from home, and the challenges of keeping essential workers safe and healthy during a global pandemic.

3. Organized labor vs. "right to work" laws
4. Strong environmental regulations vs. job creation
5. Social security vs. employer-sponsored 401k plans
6. Tax and education policies that tend to favor the wealthy and college educated vs. policies that focus on low-income groups with limited education and resources

In your day-to-day life as a manager, you may rarely have the opportunity or need to ponder these macro issues. It is nevertheless important to be mindful of the historical and political forces that are pushing and pulling you, your employees, and your organization.

THE IMPORTANT MICRO FACTORS

With the macro factors in mind, let's review the micro factors that are more likely to be the spark that leads to a breakdown in the employment relationship. At a time of hyper-partisanship, too many Americans believe that they are always right and anyone who disagrees with them or criticizes their decisions is either wrong, misinformed, or just stupid. Psychologists refer to this as the "false-consensus bias." People tend to overestimate their own opinions, actions, values, and behaviors, and devalue others' perspectives. Due to this bias, people often believe their actions and decisions are correct and normal. They believe that there is a general consensus as to the "way things are," when no such consensus exists. For example, if your social media feed has a steady stream of articles and updates about healthy eating, you may have a false consensus that everyone in your community or the country at large cares (or better yet *should* care) about healthy eating. Therefore, if someone does not care about healthy eating (or worse, embraces what you deem to be an unhealthy lifestyle), you are likely to believe they are not "normal" or that they are "wrong." Substitute healthy eating with politics or religion, and you begin to understand the power of the false-consensus bias.

The workplace is certainly not immune to this bias. In fact, it is a breeding ground for false consensus. The classic example is where upper management believes that a new policy is in the best interests of their employees without ever gauging whether in fact the employees believe the policy is a good idea.

I recall a situation a few years ago when the executive team of a company decided that because they, like many of us, could not live without obsessively checking their work email at night and on the weekends, their rank-and-file would also like the ability to do so. That year, instead of giving a Christmas bonus, the company bought every employee a smartphone. In addition to several wage and hour concerns with giving hourly nonexempt employees smartphones, the bigger problem is that the leadership team never asked themselves whether their employees wanted 24/7 access to the workplace. A few months after the "smartphone debacle" the company discontinued the program, collected the smartphones, and retroactively paid out a Christmas bonus and additional overtime.

The false-consensus bias is particularly acute when I have to tell a company's leadership that a superstar manager may have violated company policy or the law. The bias comes in when upper management has only heard positive things about this employee and believes that everyone else in the company agrees that this employee can do no wrong. This bias has unfortunately led too many intelligent and hardworking executives to believe that nearly every employment claim by an unhappy employee is frivolous. Similarly, far too many employees (often as plaintiffs in a lawsuit), particularly those who have been terminated for poor performance, believe that their manager is "out to get them" and are unable to recognize their own deficiencies. The false-consensus bias leads many disgruntled ex-employees to believe that they were "wronged," not because they have actual evidence to support their belief, but simply because it is *their* belief.

Over the course of this book, we will discuss concrete steps managers can take to become better managers and avoid costly employment disputes. In order to set the table for this discussion we will first analyze the most common culprits for the breakdown of the employment relationship and why the false-consensus bias plays such a prominent role in the workplace. Before we discuss preventative ways for you to avoid employment traps, we must first discuss what factors contribute to these problems in the first place. Where significant historical events are the macro factors that have given birth to the current legal landscape, these micro factors impact every employer, every day.

Having thought about this issue for many years, I have concluded that at least one of 10 factors (and often more than one) are usually at the root of every employment dispute. It is important that business leaders and managers acknowledge that these 10 factors exist and implement policies and procedures to deal with them head-on.

1. A Failure to Communicate: Misalignment between Employee and Manager

How many times have you left a meeting or a one-on-one with your manager or subordinate with an understanding that you had clear direction on the plan going forward, only to later be reprimanded (or do the reprimanding yourself) because you or your subordinate did not follow a "clear directive"? If you are like me, this has happened more times than you care to admit.

Epidemiologists who study a new infectious disease are often tasked with locating "Patient Zero," or the first person to have introduced a virus into the general population. HR professionals, when investigating conflict in the workplace, make every effort to delve into the past to find the first time that the relationship between an employee and their manager soured. Often the culprit is a breakdown in communication that was never properly repaired. And much like an infectious disease, if the miscommunication rapidly spreads, it often leads to a situation where the manager and employee can no longer tolerate one another. Avoiding communication mishaps by focusing on practical ways managers can better communicate with their subordinates to avoid misunderstandings and meltdowns will be covered extensively throughout this book.

2. Human Resources is Kept in the Dark

Several years ago, a company that I consult with determined that it had a serious problem: most managers were ignoring HR, which led to inconsistent policies and procedures and a slew of unnecessary lawsuits. In response, the CEO took two important steps. First, she mandated that every HR leader spend half of their day embedded with their internal clients. The immediate impact of this was that the HR team was much more present. Second, the HR VP sent every employee a red "panic button" embossed with the following statement: "NEED HELP? Contact HR!" Within six months, managers were no longer bypassing HR at every turn, and the number of employment claims dropped considerably.

It is never a good idea for a manager to adopt a "go-at-it-alone" strategy when dealing with an issue that involves HR policy. Too often, managers make decisions without consulting their HR department, resulting in confusion, lack of communication, and possible legal claims. As mentioned in Chapter 1, this book is not intended to turn every manager into an HR expert. Instead, managers will learn how to stay compliant with a myriad of employment laws and regulations, while being able to identify issues that need to be escalated immediately to HR.

When all else fails, managers faced with the decision of whether to "freestyle" an issue or bring it to the HR department's attention should opt for the latter. If an employment issue goes sideways, regardless of whether the manager bears responsibility or not, it is always best for the manager to be able to honestly say that they involved HR at the earliest practical time.

3. Ignorance is Not Bliss

Eighteenth-century poet Thomas Gray penned the famous phrase, "Where ignorance is bliss, 'tis folly to be wise." The idea that a lack of knowledge creates happiness is great for believing in the tooth fairy and that all 32 NFL teams have an equal shot at winning the Super Bowl, but is a dangerous philosophy when applied to employment law.

Both employers and employees forget that ignorance is *not* bliss. I have heard managers respond to wage and hour claims with the simple refrain: "I didn't know it was against the law to. . ." Similarly, it is not uncommon to hear an ex-employee testify that they *believed* their manager violated the law, without the faintest idea as to whether the alleged conduct was even unlawful.

The cure for ignorance is training and compliance. To effectively manage without fear, leaders need to understand the employment law landscape and incorporate best practices—many covered in this book. They also need to put their decisions under the microscope, particularly to avoid the danger of "bias creep" as discussed in Chapter 5. Employers that spend the time to educate their managers on legal compliance issues foster an environment where managers make better decisions and create less opportunity for an employee to seek legal recourse. This is the *raison d'être* why I wrote this book.

4. Gaming the System

Many employment disputes are simply the product of one manager or employee taking advantage of another. Examples of this are a rogue manager who asks employees to work off the clock so that the manager does not have to report overtime, or an employee who files a fabricated complaint to HR immediately after receiving a poor performance review. Managers and leaders in an organization need to be on the lookout for warning signs so they can identify situations where a fellow manager or a subordinate is "gaming the system."

5. Employees "Lawyer Up" Early, Sending Both Sides to Extreme Positions

Several years ago, a client received a baffling letter from a current employee's attorney. The reason for the letter was that the employee, and now her attorney, felt it was unfair and illegal that the employee received a 9 out of 10 on her annual review—which, interestingly, made her the highest performer in the department. When the in-house attorney called the employee's lawyer to ask why he wasted his time and his client's money sending out such a silly letter, the lawyer responded that his client really felt that she deserved a perfect 10.

While most disgruntled employees usually do not rush to hire an attorney every time they receive a less than perfect performance review, it is not uncommon for employees to retain a lawyer before allowing the internal grievance process to play out. When this happens, the employee and the company tend to retreat to their respective positions, which rarely works to anyone's advantage.

6. Difficulties Handling Complicated HR Matters

Most HR departments are able to independently handle 99 percent of day-to-day employment issues that come their way. It is the sticky 1 percent that often cause the biggest headaches. And when those companies do not have a "go-to" employment attorney on speed dial (either in-house or as outside counsel), the issues can get quickly out of hand. Forgetting Benjamin Franklin's famous lesson that an ounce of prevention is worth a pound of cure can cost an employer millions of dollars.

7. Companies Have Good Policies on the Books, but Forget to Follow Them

One of the first things I tell every client when I sit down with them to discuss creating or revising an employee handbook is that it is often preferable to NOT have a policy covering a particular area than to have a policy and not follow it. To put it differently, if you are going to have a written policy, it is imperative that you and the company abide by it.

This is often most acute when it comes to policies surrounding progressive discipline. Employers will often adopt a standard discipline policy with a tiered approach in dealing with performance issues (e.g., verbal warning, written warning, performance improvement plan, termination). While many companies effectively enforce such policies, they are not necessary for every organization. Savvy plaintiff's attorneys who have a bad case will look for any way to claim that the company mistreated their client. So when all else fails, if they can find examples of the company not following established policies, they will use that as "evidence" of mistreatment (e.g., "my client only received three written warnings when the policy says employees are entitled to four").

8. Lack of Quality Documentation

During a recent lecture to HR Managers, I asked the 30 participants in the room to share the single biggest "pet peeve" they have when a manager comes to them asking for permission to separate an underperforming employee. It came as no surprise to me (and should not be a surprise to you) that the number one answer was a "thin file." The conversation usually goes something like this:

Manager: Hey HR, I have this underperforming employee that I really need to fire ASAP. Do I have your permission to let him go?

HR:	Although the employee is "at will" (and can be let go any time with or without cause), what are your reasons for wanting to separate this employee?
Manager:	I can give you a million reasons. This employee is a bad apple. I have managed him for three years, and have tried everything to get him to work. I have bent over backwards but he refuses to improve and his performance is actually getting worse.
HR:	Sounds like it is time to move forward with an involuntary termination. To make sure we have all of our ducks in a row, please provide me all of the write-ups and disciplinary notes that you have kept for this employee over the past three years. It must be a pretty large file by now.
Manager:	Notes? Files? I never actually documented all of these problems. But don't worry, everyone who knows this guy agrees with me that he needs to pack his bags.
HR:	Not so fast. Before we can terminate the employee we should put him on a performance improvement plan. I really wish you had come to me earlier so that we could deal with this before you wanted to tear your hair out.

How to effectively and legally document performance issues so you have a clean and clear record to support the termination decision the next time you reach out to HR for permission to separate an employee will be addressed throughout this book.

9. Failure to Remove Underperforming Employees

The adage goes that it is usually much easier to hire 10 new employees than to let one go. Managers, like most people, tend to avoid conflict wherever possible, which often results in giving underperforming employees a free pass. This problem is often exacerbated when an underperforming employee is passed from one department to the other (or from one store or restaurant to another) like a hot potato. When this happens, the underperforming employee is never held accountable for their actions. And even worse, there is often an impression that the employee's conduct and poor performance is considered acceptable. This is particularly problematic when a manager does not want to ruffle any feathers and gives the employee a "meets expectations" review when in reality the employee should have been given a failing grade.

10. Forgetting That Human Capital is Not a Commodity

Finally, conflict in the workplace is sometimes the result of companies forgetting that employees are people with feelings, emotions, anxieties, and bills to pay. Those employers that make it a priority to approach difficult employment decisions with compassion are less likely to end up in litigation. I am not suggesting that companies should keep underperforming employees on the payroll or shy away from necessary layoffs because it will negatively impact certain employees. As we discuss in Chapter 15, however, when making these tough decisions, employers need to consider how to best communicate news of separations or layoffs—focusing on their legal responsibilities along with a healthy amount of respect and empathy.

These 10 common reasons for the breakdown in the employment relationship, along with the "macro" historical/economic issues previously discussed, help explain why employment lawsuits continue to proliferate. You may be asking yourself, with all of these factors in play, many of which you cannot possibly control, how can you manage fairly and without fear? This question poses the challenge you have as a people manager. Now that you have a solid understanding of why the relationship between employees and managers in many organizations desperately needs to be improved, you can direct your attention to what you can and will do as a manager to help heal the divide.

• • • • • • • • • • •
MANAGING WITHOUT FEAR PLAYBOOK

The Ten Micro Factors at the Root of
Most Employment Disputes

1. A failure to communicate: misalignment between employees and their managers.
2. A failure to partner with HR before a manageable personnel issue becomes an unruly employment dispute.
3. A lack of leadership training on how to monitor and enforce their own employment policies, and often a lack of training on how to foster a culture of compliance around employment law in general.
4. Employees and/or managers try to "game" the system by using employment law improperly to advance their own selfish agenda.
5. "Lawyering up" early and sending both sides to extreme positions.
6. Not consulting with experienced employment law counsel when faced with difficult HR matters.
7. Companies forgetting to follow, or simply ignoring, their own employment law policies and procedures.
8. Leaders failing to properly document performance issues.
9. Keeping underperforming employees on the job far too long.
10. Forgetting that human capital is not a commodity.

CHAPTER 3

Making Sense of the Pre-Hiring Process

Job Descriptions and Recruiting

Why do we hire employees who turn out to be underperformers? Obviously, hiring managers do not intentionally hire underperformers; it often just happens that way. Since time immemorial, employers have been on a quest for the holy grail of hiring—finding and hiring excellent and loyal employees without breaking the law in the process. In other words, they give hiring managers the tools to find the "perfect" hires while making sure managers are recruiting and hiring a diverse workforce and avoiding overt and implicit unlawful bias.

THE ALL-IMPORTANT JOB DESCRIPTION

Stop. Before you start posting jobs, interviewing candidates, and making offers, take a step back and make sure you have answered the most basic, yet all too often ignored, question: "What skills and experience am I looking for in this position?" Employers frequently post job openings without first determining how much weight they are going to place on each factor when evaluating employees. "Is education more important than job experience?" "Is work in the same industry more valuable than demonstrated success in another industry?" "Does the employee need to work an established set number of hours or is the nature of work such that the employee can work a more flexible schedule?" "Am I looking for a leader or a member of the team?" Companies that enter the recruitment and hiring process without a clear understanding of what they are looking for in their soon-to-be hired employee are bound to be disappointed with the process and risk making poor hiring decisions.

How to Draft a Quality Job Description

If there is only one takeaway from this section, it should be that before advertising a job opening it is imperative that you put together a high-quality, realistic, and legally compliant job description. Spending time crafting a thoughtful job description helps you attract the best candidates, saves time and energy reviewing resumes, and effectively markets your organization. It also helps to avoid, or at least mitigate, the risk of costly employment lawsuits.

Imagine for a moment that you just got off a call with your company's CEO, where she thanked you for your dedication and hard work and told you she is going to "reward you" with five new positions with which to grow your team. Excited by the opportunity and the kudos from the CEO, you shoot off the following email to HR:

> *Hey HR. Our amazing CEO just told me that I have three months to fill five jobs on my team. Because time is of the essence, please send me job descriptions for these positions. I would like them posted online by this time tomorrow. Thanks!*

Five minutes later, you receive the following email back from HR:

> *Hi, Manager. Excellent news about adding five FTEs to your team. We look forward to assisting you with this process. However, we need to set our expectations. If you want to recruit and hire the best candidates, we need you to provide us with a solid first draft of the job descriptions we can use to post these positions. Once you send us the job descriptions, we will then arrange a time to meet and refine them. While we are here as a resource for you, the best (and only) way to start this process is by you putting pen to paper and creating a job description. Be sure to check out Chapter 3 in the Rosenthal book for guidance. Let's plan on meeting after you finish this first phase.*

This is a common interchange between managers and HR. Managers want to hit the ground quickly, and HR reminds managers to move forward with deliberation, patience, and planning. Because a high-quality job description can lead to better hires, it is incumbent upon you to get this right. The way to get it right, or at least as close to "right" as possible, is by incorporating the following three steps.

Step 1: Elevator Pitch

Many business writers are obsessed with the metaphysical power of the elevator pitch. That is, the ability to encapsulate what you "want" (i.e., the "ask") in the 45–60 seconds it takes to get on and off an elevator. While I am of the opinion that most things in life require more than a minute to be explained, there is certainly a time and place for a deliberate elevator speech. One such occasion is when drafting a job description.

To crystallize what type of candidate you are looking to hire, you need to be able to describe the position in two to three clear sentences. Think of this as the job description's mission statement. Your elevator speech job description should include the following:

1. Job title
2. Key job duties/responsibilities
3. Core competencies necessary to be successful in this position
4. Why qualified candidates should apply for your position

Assume, for example, you want to hire a bookkeeper who has industry experience in the food service business. Because this is a relatively narrow field, your job description must stand out so it attracts the best candidates. Here are two sample elevator-pitch job descriptions for you to consider.

Example 1:   Medium-size restaurant chain looking to hire a bookkeeper with more than five years' experience and college-level accounting. Food service industry experience preferred. Full-time position, minimal travel, must be able to work independently. Only qualified candidates need apply.

Example 2:   Rapidly expanding Icelandic quick-casual restaurant chain looking for an experienced bookkeeper to manage the finances, work with management to develop best practices for financial oversight, and help us grow our business in the years to come. Interested in candidates who have successfully completed college-level courses and have experience in the restaurant business (preferably in a financial oversight role). Looking for leaders who have demonstrated the ability to perform excellent work under reasonable deadlines with amazing people. Minimal travel, competitive compensation, first-rate benefits, and plenty of tasty Icelandic cuisine.

Which elevator pitch job description is better? The first example is clear and concise. It hits all of the requirements we are looking for in our elevator speech. But would you want to apply for this position, particularly if you are already gainfully employed? Now, compare the first example with the second. The second example paints a clear picture of the "what" (a cool, rapidly growing Icelandic-themed restaurant), the "who" (a bookkeeper with solid experience), and the "why" (because you get to work with a great team with competitive pay and attractive benefits).

Clearly, the second example is what you should be working toward when drafting your elevator speech. However, and this is a big however, the elevator speech is only the first step in the process. While a well-written elevator speech job description is easy to post on LinkedIn or Twitter, it is wholly inadequate. The purpose of Step One is to stir the creative juices and help the hiring manager summarize what type of employee the manager is looking to hire. The rest of the steps take that initial vision and turn it into an actual description.

Step 2: Identify the Skills, Experiences, and Intangibles

Now that you have the position's elevator pitch, you have to get into the weeds and figure out what skills, experiences, and other intangibles you are looking for in the individuals you will ultimately want to hire. This thought exercise will help you define the position and, equally as important, will refine your expectations.

It is best to go from easiest to hardest with this exercise, which is why I encourage you to begin brainstorming the skills you "need" and the skills you "want" from a candidate. The best way to do this is by compiling a list of what a successful and realistic "day in the life" (or if you prefer, a "week in the life") will look like. Even if you are hiring for an existing position, there is value in listing out the daily duties, responsibilities, deliverables, and expectations for a successful candidate. Out of this list, you will then be able to differentiate the "needs" from the "wants."

The needs are the "essential job duties" that the position requires. In Chapter 12, we will discuss why establishing "essential job duties" at the outset is of the utmost importance. This will come into play if, in the future, your organization has to decide whether or not it is required to accommodate an employee's disability or religious tenets. For now, think of your needs list as your list of nonnegotiables. If a particular skill is truly necessary to perform the job's essential functions, then it is a "need" rather than a "want." When listing the position's essential job duties, ask yourself the following questions:

1. Does the position exist to perform the particular function? If it does, then the skill, function, or duty is essential.
2. How much time is spent performing the particular function? While not dispositive, if the employee will spend a significant amount of time performing the function, then it is likely an essential duty. For example, if an exterminator is required to spend 30 percent of the time crawling in customers' attics, then being able to crawl is an essential job duty. While this is a general rule of thumb, there are some essential job requirements that take little or no time (e.g., having a certain license or an advanced degree) but are still required.
3. Have any employees successfully performed the job without the particular skill? If the answer is "yes," then the skill is likely not essential. For example, if you think that having a BA in business is a "need" but the person being replaced, who was promoted, had a degree in art history, then a degree in business is likely a "want."

Here are some examples that show what a bona fide "need" is:

- An airline pilot must have an active pilot's license and, depending on the airline's needs, a certain number of hours flying a particular aircraft.
- A safety manager must have advanced training in occupational health and safety.
- A sanitation truck driver must have a clean driving record.
- A high school English teacher must have a master's in English literature and at least five years' teaching experience.
- A waiter on a cruise ship must be able to regularly work 10-hour days on their feet, and work and live in cramped conditions while maintaining a positive attitude.
- A manager of a large coffee chain must have at least three years of managerial experience and prior food service experience.
- A car mechanic must be able to carry up to 50 pounds, regularly stand, lift, and bend their legs and arms, and spend up to 50 percent of their shifts under a vehicle's carriage.

The "needs" are absolutes and serve as gatekeepers to ensure that only those employees who are qualified apply for and are interviewed for a position. The "wants" help the hiring manager shape the skills the manager is looking for in a candidate.

There are three categories of "wants" for a new job description. The first are those skills and experiences which are particularly desirable but do not rise to the level of essential (i.e., things that are "highly preferred" in an applicant but not absolutely necessary). In identifying the first tier of "wants," complete the following sentence: *"Highly prefer applicants who have _____."* These highly preferred skills may include education, prior experience, and industry expertise. Again, the difference between the "needs" list and the highly preferred categories is that if a candidate does not possess the latter, they are not automatically excluded from consideration.

The second tier is the "wouldn't it be nice" skills and experiences. When a hiring manager sits down to draft a job description, these are the skills that are the icing on the cake. Depending on the job, the "wouldn't it be nice" category may include the ability to speak a specific language (e.g., wouldn't it be nice if an ER nurse in San Antonio spoke Spanish), or a minimum number of years working in a particular niche (e.g., wouldn't it be nice if a sous chef for a large hotel restaurant had experience catering weddings). Neither are essential or highly preferred, but this category of skills separates candidates while helping the hiring manager articulate what skills and experiences will make a successful future employee. Certainly, as you brainstorm the list of "needs" and "wants," you might need to reshuffle the list so that a "wouldn't it be nice" migrates to a need and vice-versa. Take the nurse in the San Antonio example. Perhaps after further contemplation, you realize that the last three people who held that position were unsuccessful because they could not effectively communicate with the clinic's patient population, which is largely made up of Spanish speakers. That may prompt you to determine that conversational Spanish is an essential job duty. Of course, determining that being bilingual in English and Spanish is an essential job duty does not permit the employer to favor applicants from a particular country or individuals of a certain ethnicity. Such preferences could constitute unlawful discrimination.

The final category of skills cannot be obtained in a university program, are not associated with a license, and do not necessarily correspond with years of experience. These are the intangible traits sometimes referred to as "soft skills," that your organization has determined are the difference between decent employees and exceptional employees. Examples include demonstrated leadership, self-motivation, perseverance, being a team player, grit, etc. Depending on the job and the type of candidate your organization is looking to recruit and hire, you may spend most of the job interview process determining whether the candidate has the necessary soft skills to succeed in the position they are applying for. When posting a job application, it is important to articulate the actual soft skills needed to succeed in this role. When sorting job applicants and interviewing prospective employees, both the hiring manager and the candidate can focus on how the candidate has personified these traits in their prior work experience and training. As a cautionary note, be advised that focusing too heavily on soft skills can lead to bias creep, as we will explore in Chapter 5.

Step 3: Putting It All Together

Now that you have the elevator pitch, and have identified the essential and non-essential requirements along with the intangible "soft skills" you are looking for in a candidate, the next and final step is to draft the job description.

If you work for a small organization, you may be tasked with drafting the description with little guidance or support from HR. If you are in a larger organization, HR may provide you with considerable support and examples for the job description. Either way, the job description should be written in a clear, organized, and legal manner. Job descriptions generally should be organized around the following outline and list duties and responsibilities often using bullet points.

1. *Job Title*: Job title along with a blurb of the job description (i.e., your elevator pitch).

2. *General Job Responsibilities*: This bullet point list contains the job's day-to-day expectations and duties. Depending on the job being advertised, you may decide to keep this list very matter of fact and focused on the daily tasks or rather infuse a bit of levity. For example, if recruiting for a machinist in a furniture factory, this section will identify with specificity the responsibilities and expectations (e.g., "Ensures proper and safe operation of industrial saw and performs maintenance consistent with manufacturer's guidelines."). A tech start-up looking to hire its first office manager may, however, combine the job's daily responsibilities with a soft skill trait that the employer is looking for in a successful employee (e.g., "Work closely with the CEO in managing an office of dreamers, computer programmers, and problem-solvers, by helping to develop and execute HR polices, office workflow procedures, accounting best practices, and a positive and productive office culture."). Because this list is general in nature, it can include both the "needs" and "wants" you previously brainstormed. In articulating this list, the employer is setting expectations for the position it is hiring for, while helping prospective candidates determine if they are both qualified and interested in applying for the job.

3. *Essential Job Duties and Requirements*: I cannot stress enough how important it is to clearly list the essential job duties and requirements for the

position you are hiring. Unlike the list of general job duties and responsibilities, where you may take a vague or even whimsical approach to describing the day-to-day job responsibilities, here it is imperative that the description describes the essential duties. Recall that these are the nonnegotiable absolute requirements. If the position mandates certain physical requirements (e.g., the ability to carry 50 pounds), you must list those here. Likewise, if the position requires that the employee travel at least two weeks out of the month or must be in the office every day, you should be upfront about these requirements in the essential duties section. The same goes for education and experience. As the hiring manager, if you will not consider any candidates who lack an advanced degree in a particular field, or who do not have at least 10 years working in the industry, then be clear on this point.

4. *Compensation and Benefits*: There are three schools of thought when it comes to discussing compensation in a job description. The most common approach is not to mention it at all, or leave it intentionally ambiguous (e.g., "compensation commensurate with experience"). The second most common approach is to give a salary range. The third approach, which is gaining traction as many states demand greater transparency in compensation fueled by equal pay laws, is to inform applicants exactly what they can expect to make should they get the job. That is, if the company pays entry level employees $18 per hour for a position, then say as much in the job description. To the extent the employer prefers to offer ranges (and wants to avoid the "compensation commensurate with experience" hedge), I prefer language such as, "Company will consider salary and benefit packages in the $45,000 to $55,000 range depending on experience, skills, and education." A word of caution: avoid including "prior salary" as a factor in determining an employee's compensation as it is illegal to ask for that information in some states and creates problems in others. On a related note, the job description should clearly state whether the employee will be treated as "exempt" from overtime or "nonexempt" from overtime (i.e., entitled to receive overtime compensation).

5. *Educational Requirements*: If there are specific minimum educational requirements for the position, identify the requirements.

Step 4: Quick Legal Audit

Before you post the job description online or give the green light to your recruiter to start hunting for qualified candidates, it is imperative that you conduct a quick "legal audit" to make sure the job description is legally compliant. While certain jobs will require a more comprehensive legal audit, which may require assistance from an attorney, most legal audits can be done by the frontline manager with a final review from HR. As you conduct this audit, answer the following questions:

1. *Does the job description contain a clear Equal Employment Opportunity (EEO) statement?* If it does not, you should consider adding an EEO statement at the end of the description.[1]
2. *Does the job description identify all of the bona fide essential job duties for the position, including all physical requirements?* If there are duties listed as "essential" when they are merely preferred, it is important to recalibrate the list.
3. *Does the job description unnecessarily use gendered terms?* To avoid the appearance that the position is intended for one gender over the other, it is important to scrub the description of any terms that suggest a gender preference (e.g., foreman, paperboy, cocktail waitress, jack-of-all-trades, etc.).
4. *Could the job description as written have a disparate impact on certain individuals who are not members of a "favored group?"* As we discuss in greater detail in Chapter 10, disparate impact discrimination is unintentional discrimination, where certain policies or practices appear on their face to be neutral but result in a disproportionate negative impact on certain groups. For example, unless there is a legitimate business reason, a position that requires applicants to be at least 5'2" tall could have a disparate impact on female applicants because about a third of all women in the United States are shorter than 5'2" while less than 13 percent of men are unable to satisfy that height requirement.
5. *Is the position properly classified as exempt or nonexempt?* Discussed in greater detail in Chapter 13, properly classifying an employee as "overtime exempt" (or simply "exempt") or nonexempt (i.e., entitled to overtime among other benefits) has major ramifications on how the employee

works and is paid. Misclassifying an employee can create considerable risk to the organization. Because there are widely different standards depending on the state the employee works in, this is one area of employment law in which you should always defer to HR or your trusted employment law attorney.

Congratulations! You have now taken the necessary steps to craft an accurate, comprehensive, legally compliant, and perhaps even enticing, job description. The next jaunt on the hiring journey is the all-important, although often overlooked from a legal compliance standpoint, recruiting process.

THE RECRUITING PROCESS

Paraphrasing Albert Einstein, effective and lawful recruiting is 99 percent perspiration and 1 percent inspiration. Whether your company uses third-party recruiters, internal resources, web-based solutions, job postings, word-of-mouth, or a combination of all five methods, recruiting your next hire is often a lengthy, time-consuming, and frustrating process. While I have been involved in many hiring decisions for my own law firms and various non-profit organizations (and when advising clients as an employment attorney), I am certainly not a recruiting guru. If you are looking for how to master the art of recruiting, there are likely better resources out there. Because the ultimate goal of this book is how to manage without fear and avoid getting sued, however, it is important to touch upon the legal requirements of the recruiting process.

Lawful recruiting involves many of the same themes we previously covered when discussing job descriptions. There are, however, several aspects that are unique to the recruiting process. Here are three lessons every manager involved in recruiting should be mindful of going forward.

Lesson 1: Don't use social media to illegally focus on certain groups to the disadvantage of other "protected" groups.

Unless you have been sequestered in a cave in the Azores since about 2012, you are obviously aware of the tremendous impact social media, and in particular Facebook and LinkedIn, have had on virtually every aspect of our lives. Social media affects how we find love, reconnect with our middle school classmates, buy a car, consume the news, vote for president, and find a job. It has transformed, disrupted, and improved our lives. Savvy employers and recruiting websites jumped on the social media train years ago. And now, for most employers, using social media to attract the best candidates is no longer just one option, but is now a key component of the recruiting process. According to a recent study by the Society for Human Resource Management (SHRM), over 80 percent of companies (as of 2015) use social media in recruiting applicants.[2] Given that you and your company are likely already using social media in recruiting, it is important to take a step back and see if you are engaging with social media in a legal way.

The ability to connect with billions of people exists because internet companies from the earliest incarnations of Google and Yahoo to the present have figured out how to monetize every click. Companies and advertisers in particular have, in turn, become very sophisticated in micro-targeting which individuals see their content. While this practice is the lifeblood of the commercial internet, using micro-targeting for recruiting can also lead to discrimination.

Consider the following hypothetical situation. Say you are the regional manager of a growing hipster boxing yoga gym franchise that started in Los Angeles, focusing on the Hollywood set (i.e., young and beautiful aspiring actors who moonlight as waiters), and is now spreading its Rocky-themed hot yoga classes across the Midwest. You need to immediately hire gym managers, Boxga (a portmanteau of boxing and yoga) instructors, and front desk receptionists in Chicago, Milwaukee, and Ann Arbor. Time is of the essence. First, you try the traditional methods of recruiting. You post jobs online, blast your personal network with annoying emails and social media posts, and hire a recruiter to source some of these jobs. Alas, you have made little headway, and your boss Ivan Drago Namaste is giving you a month to staff up these gyms or he will have to go in a "different direction."

Being the marketing pro that you are, you log onto Facebook and create an advertisement that micro-targets the demographics you believe are most likely to work in a boxing/yoga gym. First, you select the users you want to see the advertisement based on location (focusing only on specific zip codes that happen to be in largely upper middle class and predominantly white neighborhoods). Second, you select users who have an interest in boxing, yoga, or both (the rarest of birds). Next, you ask the Facebook algorithm to further drill down and target (1) women who "like" a certain Canadian company that sells amazingly durable, very fashionable, and rather pricey black stretchy pants; and (2) men who follow celebrities that take selfies while performing yoga moves in their skivvies. And finally, you further target your advertisements to the likely demographic of your future customers (e.g., ages 18–35). After telling Facebook exactly who you want to see your advertisements, you sit back and wait for the applicants to roll in. And roll they do. Your strategy works very well. You now have a crop of employees at your gyms who have the "look" and "feel" you were aiming for when you started this process. All is good. That is, until your boss Ivan calls you into his office along with the head of HR to tell you that the company just got hit with a class action lawsuit alleging that the company engaged in discriminatory hiring practices.

At that point, you learn that aspects of your micro-targeting strategy crossed the line from legal recruiting to illegal discrimination. While it was completely permissible to target individuals who, at least on social media, profess an interest in boxing, yoga, or both, targeting zip codes in specific cities that are predominantly white is problematic (targeting entire cities would have been okay). Another problem was limiting your search to women who are fans of an expensive yoga clothing company, and men who tend to only follow white influencers. While you did not think about the ethnicity and age when you ran this search, legally speaking you should have known that by limiting your search in this manner, it would result in a skewed applicant pool that trended overwhelmingly young, white, and wealthy. And while this micro-targeting could pass muster if you were able to justify a nondiscriminatory reason for selecting these two groups, there is no justification for illegally narrowing the age, which excluded potential applicants over 40 (so-called "older workers"). Although you believed you were carrying out your boss's orders and certainly did not intend to discriminate against anyone, these discriminatory practices (along with the lawsuit and bad press) result in your immediate termination.

In 2016 and 2017, Facebook was hit with several lawsuits by civil rights groups and unions, claiming that the social media giant was illegally allowing companies to improperly micro-target users in violation of both equal opportunity employment as well as housing laws. At issue were a number of advertisements—including, ironically, an advertisement by Facebook's own recruiting department—that targeted users by their age. The lawsuits also cited several companies in male-dominated professions, including truck driving and manufacturing, who were targeting their job postings so that only men received their advertisements. To its credit, Facebook recognized the serious problem with allowing micro-targeting in the employment space and implemented policies to prevent third parties from misusing Facebook's algorithm.

The key takeaway is that when devising a recruiting strategy (whether online or in person), employers must be careful that their recruiting efforts do not unintentionally use discriminatory criteria.

Lesson 2: Avoid asking candidates for information that impermissibly seeks out or weeds out candidates based on protected characteristics.

As a general rule, if you are not allowed to ask a question to a candidate during an interview, you can't ask the same question during the general recruitment and initial screening process. For this reason, recruiters must be careful about what "lenses" they apply to narrow their recruitment strategy. Here are a few "do's" and "don'ts" to guide you during the recruitment process.

- DO structure your recruitment around your company's equal opportunity principles.
- DO advertise job openings internally and externally.
- DON'T artificially limit the folks you recruit. If you spent the time drafting a high-quality and legal job description, your recruiters have a roadmap of the essential job duties you are looking for in that position. For example, if you are recruiting for a role that requires a certain educational level or specific industry experience, use those essential job duties as a "fishing net" when recruiting. At the same time, avoid having recruiters limit their pool by using the "wouldn't it be nice" list of skills and experiences.

- DO call out potential bias in the recruitment process, in particular implicit bias, and implement strategies to prevent bias creep (Chapter 5 is devoted exclusively to the perils of implicit bias and strategies to remove bias from personnel decisions). Just because the position you are recruiting for has historically had a certain "look" (e.g., gender, age, family background, marital status, etc.), this should not be the barometer in recruiting the next candidate.

- DO make sure your recruiters have a strong understanding of the position, the organization's culture, and the team to which the recruiter is looking to add. At the same time, the recruiter does not need to have all of the answers. A strong recruiter will not speak out of turn, but instead, will bring back questions to the hiring manager and HR.

- DO make sure your recruiter understands and abides by state law. As discussed in the next chapter, several states have special requirements regarding what an employer can and cannot ask a candidate during the application and interview process.

- DO abide by your company's policy regarding checking an applicant's social media presence. Some companies have strict policies that prohibit managers from combing through a candidate's social media life, out of a concern that the hiring manager may learn information about the candidate's personal life that is of no consequence to whether the candidate will be a good employee. This knowledge could taint the manager's perception of the candidate, setting up a potential discrimination claim (e.g., learning that the applicant lives an entirely legal yet by societal standards "alternative" lifestyle). Other companies have a policy that only HR can search a candidate's social media footprint, to ensure that information learned on social media is not improperly factored into hiring decisions.

Lesson 3: You may be responsible for your third-party recruiter's misdeeds.

Employers can be liable for a headhunter's screw-ups. If a third-party recruiter engages in illegal tactics to pursue or weed out certain candidates, liability could belong to the company that engaged the recruiter. As a manager who may be far removed from the decision to hire a third-party recruiting firm to assist in a job search, it is important to be mindful of several red flags so you can avoid having to answer for a recruiter's misdeeds:

- *Red Flag #1:* A recruiter tells you that they are going to focus on specific groups that you know could lead to discriminatory hiring (e.g., focusing on candidates of a particular age range, avoiding candidates from a certain part of town, etc.). Even when a recruiter is savvy enough not to explicitly call out their discriminatory ways, a suitable wink or nod should launch your internal red flags.
- *Red Flag #2:* The recruiter relays information about certain candidates that you know you shouldn't know and have no bearing on the individual's ability to be a successful employee. For example, if the recruiter tells you that a candidate is pregnant, married, gay, or Muslim, that should be a red flag to you that the recruiter has clearly crossed the line.
- *Red Flag #3:* The recruiter lies to candidates. If during the interview process you find out that the recruiter lied to the person you are interviewing, that should raise concerns about the recruiter's proclivity for honesty and integrity. While this does not necessarily translate to discriminatory conduct, it could be a sign that the recruiter is cutting corners.
- *Red Flag #4:* The recruiter is only sending you candidates with a certain "look." One way to spot potential bias in the hiring process is if all, or a vast majority, of the candidates you receive that were already vetted by the recruiter are a homogeneous bunch (i.e., only men of a certain age, only Asians, only women under 30, etc.). The way to ensure that the recruiter is not engaging in overt discrimination or perpetuating decisions based on implicit bias is by asking the recruiter to be very clear and transparent about the steps they took to build a diverse pool of candidates. If the recruiter is unable to offer a credible response, a more comprehensive strategy and further conversation is needed. Just because the recruiter sends you a crop of candidates that have a similar "look" does not necessarily mean that there is anything amiss. But as a leader who is trained in the art of employment law compliance, this should at least prompt a discussion for you to confirm that that the recruiter is performing a lawful search.

○ ○ ○ ○ ○ ○ ○ ○ ○ ○ ○
MANAGING WITHOUT FEAR PLAYBOOK

How to Draft a Quality Job Description

Step One: Develop a captivating "elevator pitch" for the job.

Step Two: Identify the skills, experiences, and intangibles you are looking for in the employee. Develop a clear list of the position's "essential job duties" by listing all of the skills, physical requirements, and "nonnegotiables" you are looking for. Then, for each one, ask the following three questions:

1. Does the position exist in order to perform the particular function? If the answer is "yes" then it is likely an essential job duty.
2. How much time is spent performing the particular function? The more time spent on that function means the more likely it is essential.
3. Have any employees successfully performed the job without the particular skill? If the answer is "yes" then it is likely not essential.

Step Three: Put it all together by including the following information:

1. Job title
2. General job responsibilities
3. Essential job duties and requirements
4. Compensation and benefits
5. Educational requirements

Step Four: Perform a quick "legal audit" by asking the following questions:

1. Does the job description contain an Equal Employment Opportunity statement?
2. Are the duties listed as "essential" truly essential, including all physical requirements?
3. Does the job description contain unnecessary gendered terms?
4. Could the job description have a disparate impact on individuals in "protected" groups?
5. Is the position properly classified as overtime "exempt" (i.e., not entitled to overtime) or "nonexempt" (i.e., entitled to overtime and other wage and hour benefits)?

CHAPTER 4

Conducting a Lawful Job Interview and Selecting the Right Candidate

Job interviews are the most important aspect of the hiring process. If one were to look for the weakest link in the hiring process chain, where leaders are at the greatest risk of not complying with the law and of making poor decisions that can haunt them for years to come, it would be the job interview. This is due to a variety of factors.

First and foremost, a good job interview fosters spontaneity and human connection. If we only hired employees based on an algorithm—taking into account the applicant's education, prior experience, and answers to a variety of standardized questions, without ever actually meeting and speaking with the candidate—in most cases, this would result in a mismatch between the new employee and their new employer. While the vast majority of colleges and universities in the United States can get away with accepting a select number of individuals out of a large pool of applicants without ever actually interviewing the students, such a strategy would not translate into the work environment. In the workplace, interpersonal connections, work and life experience, and verbal communication skills usually far outweigh anything an algorithm can tell hiring managers about an applicant. Of course, the very spontaneity and human connection that is the hallmark of the interview process can, if unchecked, result in bias and discrimination.

Second, all too often individual managers who conduct job interviews are insufficiently prepared to stay within legal boundaries. If you consider yourself to be in this camp, don't fret. After reading this chapter, you will be squarely in the group of managers who are well trained on what they can and cannot ask during a job interview.

Third, selecting employees who will hold up their end of the grand bargain—the theory that if the company treats them well during their employment, they will reciprocate and be loyal and productive workers and good company citizens—is really hard. One of the first things I do when representing a company in a lawsuit filed by a former employee is interview the hiring manager and ask about the decision to bring the ex-employee on in the first place. In response, I often hear, "If only I paid attention to the red flags during the interview, we would not be in this mess." Being able to identify potential red flags while avoiding implicit bias is not an easy task.

And finally, job interviews are particularly fertile grounds for employment law violations because, as hiring managers, we often find it difficult to put our finger on the exact reason we prefer one candidate over another. This can lead to false accusations of discrimination. Simply put, we tend to focus so much on what we can and cannot say during a job interview (see below) that we often forget the second part of the equation, explaining *why* we are apt to select one candidate over another. For this reason, we will focus on how to properly verbalize our entirely lawful and above-board hiring decisions at the end of this chapter.

TEN TOPICS TO AVOID WHEN INTERVIEWING A JOB APPLICANT

Conducting a legally compliant job interview is not difficult, but it requires a healthy dose of intentionality. As a starting off point, every interviewer must be mindful of their role in upholding the organization's equal opportunity policies and the law (sample interview questions to help managers make the best choice in selecting new hires can be found in other resources). Because this book focuses on how to navigate the law, our attention will be on what *not* to ask when sitting down with a candidate. While some cities and states are more restrictive on what information an employer can ask during the hiring process, you are well on your way to conducting a lawful interview if you avoid the topics below. It should be noted that for many, but not all, of these topics, there are exceptions to the general rule where in limited circumstances it is permissible to carefully broach some of these subjects. In an abundance of caution, however, it is worthwhile to first seek advice from your HR representative or in-house legal department before you jump into potentially dangerous waters.

Topic 1: "Do They Plan on Having Children, and If So, How Will They Juggle Work and Home Responsibilities"

Several years ago I received a call from the CEO of a 250-employee and rapidly growing consulting company who had a bone to pick with me. The CEO had recently attended an executive employment law training where I lectured on preventing harassment and discrimination in the workplace. The CEO, who by way of background had a PhD in economics, took issue with the fact that I told him and the other participants that it is never permissible to ask a candidate during a job interview about the candidate's childcare situation, nor is it permissible to ask whether the candidate intends to have children in the near future.

According to the CEO, his company spends more than $75,000 recruiting, on-boarding, and training every new hire. Furthermore, he told me that it takes about a year for a new employee to actually be profitable. The problem, he relayed to me, is that within the past two years, three highly compensated employees had gone on extended maternity leaves within the first year of their employment, which "caused considerable disruption." Another three employees, who had been with the company for less than two years, decided not to return from their baby-bonding leaves. In light of this situation, the CEO asked whether it was reasonable to ask candidates if they intend to have kids in the next few years and, if so, who the primary caretaker would be. The CEO assured me that he would ask this question to both men and women. He made it clear that he would not necessarily reject any candidates based on this information, but that having it would be useful when making staffing decisions. He strenuously argued that it is no different than asking a recent college graduate how long they intend to work before returning to graduate school to obtain their MBA or pursue another advanced degree. The CEO believed that it is unfair to prohibit questions concerning an applicant's commitment to staying with the company. Applicants can take a job knowing full well that they will likely leave for an extended period within the first few years and may even decide not to return after they have kids.

After letting the CEO vent, I asked him four questions. First, taking his argument to a logical conclusion, I asked him if it made "economic sense" to have every applicant submit to a comprehensive medical and psychological screening along with a genetic consult, so that he can weed out any applicants who are predisposed to cancer, heart disease, depression, and anxiety? Expectedly, he responded that of course that would be far too intrusive, and employers have no right to such personal and sensitive information.

Second, I asked the CEO to calculate the percentages of his employees, broken down by gender, who have taken an extended leave of absence (in excess of one month) to take care of a new child. He immediately responded that all but one of the employees he mentioned were women. He reluctantly acknowledged that such a line of inquiry would disproportionately impact women, even if he asked the question to every job applicant.

Third, I asked the CEO (who claims to be a strong proponent of diversity and inclusion) if he believes there are any societal benefits to making sure that employers avoid any questions about an applicant's highly personal decisions around family planning. He reluctantly conceded that if he asked such questions (or if he assumed that a certain applicant was more likely to have a short tenure with the company), he would be sending the wrong message to his female coworkers and future employees, along with his valued clients. The message would be that the company is not a welcoming place for employees with young children. As a CEO who prides himself on being a first-rate employer, he acknowledged that such questions would not only be inappropriate and illegal, but would likely result in fewer women joining the company.

And finally, once I had made my point, I reminded him that asking such questions are against the law. I asked him if he were inclined to break the law would he be prepared to spend hundreds of thousands of dollars defending an illegal hiring practice? By that point his "cold, economic brain" (his words, not mine) turned off, and he fully acknowledged that such questions are way out of bounds.

The basic lesson here is that absent extraordinary circumstances (e.g., where a currently pregnant woman could not safely perform the job), it is never permissible to ask candidates about their family planning. Similarly, while it is permissible to ask applicants if they have reliable transportation to and from work, it is never permissible to ask candidates about their childcare arrangements. As a general rule of thumb, any discussions regarding children, pregnancy, and future leaves of absence should be avoided while conducting a job interview. If a candidate brings up children during an interview, the best course of action (for a manager educated in the art of employment law) is to redirect the conversation and, if appropriate, remind the candidate that the company has a very robust equal employment opportunity policy.

The bigger lesson from my conversation with the CEO is that employment law is far from a free-market Ayn Rand utopia (or dystopia depending on your worldview). Rather, the laws governing the employment relationship are a colorful patchwork of labor economics, public policy, civil rights, politics, and business objectives. As you read the rest of this book, you may develop the belief that certain employment law requirements make little if any business sense. And while you may be correct in certain circumstances, it is important not to confuse what is "right" for business (i.e., maximizing profit and efficiency) with what is legal with respect to the employer-employee relationship.

Topic 2: "You Look Much Younger Than You Probably Are"

Stay away from questions about an applicant's age. Absent a bona fide minimum age requirement (e.g., over 21 to work in a bar), there is no reason to inquire or speculate about a candidate's age. Most leaders are sophisticated enough to know that asking candidates pointblank how old they are, or making an inane offhand comment such as "You look good for your age" (a two-fold problem, commenting on both age and appearance) is entirely unacceptable.

What is less intuitive is asking seemingly innocuous questions that unintentionally touch upon a candidate's age. For example, asking candidates what year they graduated from high school can give rise to an age discrimination allegation, even if you only asked the question because you wanted to know if the candidate overlapped with a friend or relative who went to the same high school.

Another common *faux pas* on the age front is addressing the elephant in the room. Consider the following scenario. You are the manager of a popular shoe store located in a mall that caters to customers between the ages of 13 and 23. Your district manager asks you to interview two candidates for a sales position. The first is a recent high school graduate with two years of solid retail experience (you know that because the candidate tells you and it is obvious that he is barely 18 years old). This candidate looks like many of your customers, and frankly looks like you a few years ago (in this hypothetical, you are not a day over 25). The second candidate is a woman who appears to be in her mid-50s (at least, she looks like your mom who just turned 55). This candidate has worked in retail her entire life and has a proven track record in shoe sales. The more experienced candidate is clearly your first choice, but you are concerned that the "age barrier" will pose a problem. You decide to address your concerns head on. First, you ask whether the candidate is concerned that the significant age gap between herself and the store's customers will hinder her ability to be successful. While you did not intend the question to be offensive, and it certainly would make an interesting business experiment (are teenagers more or less likely to buy Air Jordan's from a 55-year-old experienced saleswoman as compared to an 18 year old with little experience), the question is out-of-bounds because it calls out the candidate's age. The fact that the candidate is significantly older than her potential customers is of no consequence.

Next, having already broken the seal, you ask your second burning question: "Have you ever had a supervisor who was significantly younger than you, and if so, how did you respond to that challenge?" The problem with this question is not just that it calls out the candidate's age (and the significant age discrepancy between the manager and candidate), but that it also shines a light on the manager's own potential insecurities about having to manage an employee who is twice his age. There *may* in fact be real challenges that will need to be addressed down the road if the candidate is hired and has a difficult time taking guidance from a much younger manager. Any such fears or concerns, however, and the implicit bias that stems from such concerns, must not cloud the hiring process.

Topic 3: Do Not Bring up an Applicant's Religion, and Never Assume That You Will Be Unable to Accommodate a Candidate's Religious Needs Based on How the Candidate Looks

In 2008, 17-year-old Samantha Elauf applied for a job selling kids clothing at a store operated by Abercrombie & Fitch at the Woodland Hills Mall in Tulsa, Oklahoma. Elauf is a practicing Muslim who proudly wears a hijab (headscarf) outside of the house. Prior to applying for the job, Elauf spoke with one of the managers at the store about her hijab. The manager said it should not be a problem for her to wear the hijab if she was hired, as long as it was not a black hijab, as that would not fit within Abercrombie's dress code policy.

After being interviewed for a sales position (salespeople are referred to as "models"), the assistant store manager was keen on offering Elauf the job. She was concerned, however, that Elauf's hijab would conflict with Abercrombie's (since revised) "Look Policy"—the dress code that prohibits among other attire, employees from wearing "caps." Because the Look Policy promoted and showcased Abercrombie's unique brand, employees who did not abide by the Look Policy (which, among other things, required wearing Abercrombie's clothing), were subject to disciplinary action up to and including termination.

According to court records, Abercrombie's policy at the time was to instruct "store managers not to assume facts about prospective employees in job interviews and, significantly, not to ask applicants about their religion." To the extent questions arose about the Look Policy or a candidate asked for a modification (based on a religious practice), the manager was expected to contact human resources or her direct supervisor who could "grant accommodations if doing so would not harm the brand."

The assistant manager did as she was trained to do, and reached out to her store manager for guidance. The store manager was not helpful in this regard, so the assistant manager reached out to the district manager (DM) to see how she should proceed.

Lesson 1:   *The manager dropped the ball.*

Lesson 2:   *The assistant manager should have contacted HR directly.*

According to court records, the assistant manager told the DM that she believed Elauf wore the headscarf because of her faith—a most obvious inference. In turn, the DM said that wearing a headscarf violates the Look Policy, and directed the assistant manager not to hire Elauf.

Lesson 3:   *The DM was ill-informed and subjected the company to significant liability.*

The DM then instructed the assistant manager to change the interview score she had given Elauf so it would look like the assistant manager did not want to hire Elauf in the first place.

Lesson 4:   *Covering up discrimination is entirely improper.*

The U.S. Equal Employment Opportunity Commission (EEOC) represented Elauf and filed a lawsuit against Abercrombie alleging religious discrimination. At the trial, Elauf testified that she felt "disrespected because of [her] religious beliefs." The jury agreed that Elauf was discriminated against and awarded her $20,000.

On appeal, the intermediary court overturned judgment in Elauf's favor on the grounds that an employer cannot be liable for discrimination for failing to accommodate a religious practice *unless and until* the applicant provides the employer with "actual knowledge" of their need for a religious accommodation. The appellate court reasoned that employers can choose not to hire an applicant because the applicant is wearing certain religiously identifiable clothing, *unless* the candidate verbalizes that they (1) are engaged in a particular practice, (2) did so for religious reasons, and (3) require an accommodation to do (or continue to do) the job in question. For example, in this case, Elauf would need to verbalize her need for an accommodation from the Look Policy in order to work for the Company and exercise her religious rights. The appellate court noted that because Elauf never called attention to the fact that she wore her hijab for religious reasons (as opposed to cultural or fashion reasons), Abercrombie could not have engaged in religious discrimination against her because the company had no way of knowing *why* she wore her hijab. The court noted that the EEOC's own guidelines encourage employers not to ask questions during a job interview about religion, and that an employer's obligations to accommodate an employee only arise *after* the employer is formally put on notice.

Later, in an 8-1 decision, the U.S. Supreme Court overturned the appellate court's decision. Writing for the Court, the late Justice Antonin Scalia skewered the court of appeals for taking such a small-minded view of an employer's duties to accommodate an applicant. The Court held that the law prohibits an employer from taking action "with the motive of avoiding the need for accommodating a religious practice." In this case, the evidence was unambiguous. Abercrombie did not hire Elauf because they did not want to have to determine whether they needed to make an accommodation for her.

There are three main takeaways from the Elauf case. First, when making hiring decisions it is never permissible for an employer to forgo its duty to engage in the interactive process by simply rejecting the applicant out-of-hand. This lesson holds true anytime a candidate who may need an accommodation applies for a job.

Second, managers must view a candidate's religious differences—just as they would view any other applicant's race, gender, sexual orientation, and national origin—as entirely irrelevant to hiring decisions. One of the hallmarks of the American experiment is that we are a nation that prides itself on religious freedom and tolerance. Our workplaces must be equally welcoming to religious differences.

And finally, managers should be prepared to either answer questions as they come up about religious accommodations (or any accommodations for that matter) or defer to HR, but they should never wing it. The Elauf case is a bit unusual. In my experience, candidates will often bring up the accommodation request during the interview process. Taking the facts from that case, let's suppose the manager conducting Elauf's interview reviewed the Look Policy with every applicant during their interview. Let's also assume that the manager asked every applicant whether or not they had any concerns with the Look Policy. Had Elauf then asked, "*Will I be violating the policy if I wear my traditional Muslim head scarf?*" that would have invited a conversation between the manager and Elauf on this topic. If the manager knew that

Company policy allowed accommodation, as long as the employee wears clothing that fits within the Abercrombie style and the headscarf would be worn for religious reasons, the manager could say as much. Of course, if the manager was not entirely clear about the policy, she could respond, "*Great question. Let me check with HR and get back to you ASAP. I want to be sure to provide you with the right answer to your important question.*"

The next time you have an opportunity to chat with your HR representative, you may want to ask about how the company has traditionally handled religious accommodation issues. If you really want to impress your HR business partner, you can specifically ask about the following common scenarios:

1. Modifying schedules for Sabbath observance
2. Modifying schedules for specific religious holidays
3. Dress code accommodations (hijabs, kippahs, turbans, etc.)
4. Polices around facial hair

Your HR partner will likely share with you how they have addressed requests for accommodations in the past, and/or times when the company has determined that a proposed accommodation was either deemed "unreasonable" or would create an "undue hardship" for the employer.

There is one final note. If you work for a religious organization (church, synagogue, religious order), and the role you are hiring for has a "Bona Fide Occupational Qualification" (BFOQ) that mandates adherence to a certain faith (e.g., priest or Sunday school religious teacher), it is generally permissible under limited circumstances to ask a candidate about their faith. As with any issue that is close to the line, it is important to seek out advice from HR and legal counsel before asking about or considering any protected classification when making hiring decisions.

Topic 4: Politics Have No Place in the Interview Room

Asking applicants during a job interview about their political views is rarely warranted or appropriate. As of the first edition of this book, there is no federal law prohibiting questions about an applicant's political views, nor are there any federal laws protecting employees from discrimination based on their political views. Several states, however, have enacted statutes prohibiting employers from taking adverse employment actions against employees for engaging in lawful external political activities. The general prohibition against discussing politics during a job interview is that knowing an applicant's political views can have an undue positive or negative (but usually unfair) impact on whether the applicant is offered a job. As we will discuss in the next chapter, opening the door to an applicant's political views can easily trigger implicit and explicit bias. This is not to say that political discourse should be censored in the workplace. There is certainly a time and place for *coworkers* to have candid and civil political conversations. But the key here is that such conversations should only take place between coworkers, not between hiring managers and applicants.

Topic 5: Feel Free to Discuss an Applicant's Military Experience, but Never Ask about Why They Left the Military

This is a simple line of reasoning to follow. If you see that an applicant served in the military, you can certainly ask about the candidate's experiences and lessons learned while in uniform. However, with few exceptions, it is best to avoid questions regarding the circumstances under which the applicant was discharged from the military.

Topic 6: An Applicant's Sexuality and Gender Identity Is Irrelevant

This is another no-brainer. There is no reason to ever ask an applicant about their sexual orientation. Period. Whether an applicant is LGBTQ+ (lesbian, gay, bisexual, transgender, questioning/queer, "plus" other sexual identities including pansexual, asexual, and allies) or straight is irrelevant to the question at the heart of every job interview: does this individual have the requisite skill, experiences, and grit to be an excellent employee? In June of 2020, the U.S. Supreme Court in *Bostock v. Clayton County, Georgia* issued one of the most important civil rights decisions in the last decade. In *Bostock*, the Court held that Title VII of the Civil Rights Act of 1964 prohibits government and private employers from discriminating based on an employee's or applicant's sexual orientation or sexual identity. While one can only hope Congress will explicitly add sexual orientation and sexual identity to existing civil rights laws, it is now illegal for the vast majority of employers (religious institutions excluded) to discriminate against LGBTQ+ individuals.

One issue that has come up for many of my clients over the past several years is what accommodations should be made at the interview stage and during the course of the employment relationship if an applicant/employee is transgender, a cross-dresser, gender nonconforming, or gender fluid/nonbinary. Using precise and respectful language when discussing gender identity and expression in the workplace is extremely important. It is, therefore, imperative that leaders have a solid understanding of the specific nomenclature used by the LGBTQ+ community:

- **Sex:** When discussing sexual orientation and gender identity, the term "sex" is the medical classification of a person as "male" or "female" at birth. Sex is what is written on a birth certificate, usually based on the baby's external anatomy.
- **Gender Identity:** A person's deeply held sense of their gender. For transgender individuals, their identity does not match their sex. While society typically views gender identity as binary (male/female), gender identity can be fluid (i.e., "nonbinary") for some people.
- **Gender Expression:** The external manifestation of a person's gender as expressed by the person's name, the pronouns used (he/she/they/ze or zie, him/her/them/hir, his/hers/theirs/hirs), their clothing, and behaviors, etc.
- **Sexual Orientation:** The gender(s) a person is physically and emotionally attracted to. To be clear, gender identity and sexual orientation are not the same thing. A transgender person may be straight, gay, or bisexual. If a person transitions from male to female, and is attracted only to men, she would identify as a straight woman.
- **Transgender:** A broad term for people whose gender identity and/or expression differ from the "sex" they were assigned at birth. Depending on their individual circumstances, some transgender folks take hormones or undergo surgery as part of their transition, while others simply modify their gender expression.

- **Cross-dresser:** A person who wears clothing associated with the opposite sex, typically a man who wears women's clothing and makeup. Unlike a transgender individual, a cross-dresser typically does not want to permanently alter their sex.

- **Transition:** The often lengthy and complicated process of transitioning from the sex assigned at birth to the opposite sex. The transition process often involves medical procedures (e.g., hormones, sex reassignment surgery, etc.), interpersonal changes (e.g., telling family and coworkers to use different pronouns, outwardly identifying as a different gender, etc.), and legal changes (e.g., name change, new identification, etc.).

- **Gender Nonconforming:** Used to describe people whose gender expression differs from societal understandings of what is "masculine" and what is "feminine." Just because someone is gender nonconforming, does not mean they are transgender.

- **Nonbinary/Genderqueer:** This describes individuals whose gender identity and/or expression exists outside of the male/female buckets. This can mean that they see themselves as existing on a spectrum between men and women, or entirely outside of traditional gender norms and definitions.

Let's consider two thoughts before we discuss concrete steps leaders can enact to make their workplaces inclusive for all employees regardless of sexual orientation and identity.

First, this is a complicated area of employment law. When gender identity/expression issues arise in the workplace, leaders need to partner early and often with their human resources departments to ensure that they are complying with their company's EEO policy and the law.

Second, I am not naïve to the fact that some people are uncomfortable with the notion that employers should be required to make accommodations for transgender employees. I also recognize that some readers may have cultural and/or religious aversions to people who do not fit squarely into conventional gender roles. If you happen to fall into this category—or have colleagues who do—you are certainly entitled to your own *personal* beliefs on this issue. Unless you work for a religious institution, however, you must separate your personal beliefs from your obligations as a leader. Now that we have that out of the way, let's discuss the most common accommodations for transgender individuals when they apply for a position with your company.

First and foremost, it goes without saying that it is important to treat every person who takes the time to apply and interview for a job with respect and dignity. Obviously, unless the applicant brings up gender identity during the interview, conduct the interview just like you would conduct any other interview. Easy enough.

So what happens if the applicant's gender identity does come up? Here are a few simple accommodations to keep in your back pocket:

- **Pronouns:** If it is not obvious to you whether the applicant identifies as male, female, or nonbinary, and the applicant does not specify a preferable pronoun at the interview stage, avoid pronouns altogether. In writing, refer to the applicant either by the applicant's name or using gender neutral terms. You may have noticed that when speaking about a generic person such as an "applicant" or "employee" who is not identified as a man or woman, I have either avoided using pronouns altogether (i.e., not using "he" or "she" or the dreaded "he or she"), or used "they" as a singular pronoun. Use of "they" to refer to a single individual may be a bit jarring to some readers, particularly those of us (me included) who were taught in school to always use "him" or "her" to identify an indefinite person of any gender (e.g., "A competent manager should not hide *his* disdain for sloppy writing."). However substituting "they" (or "them" or "themselves") for single pronouns has been acceptable since the 14th century and, of late, has become widely adopted by writers of standard English.
- **Bathrooms:** If the interviewee (or employee) needs to use the facilities, let the individual choose where they feel most comfortable.
- **Uniforms:** This is a bit trickier and requires a case-by-case analysis. As a general rule of thumb, for those companies that have gender-specific uniforms (a rarity today), allow the employee to wear the uniform of the gender that they most associate with. Whether or not to require that a cross-dressing employee "choose" one gender identity while at work and stick with it is for HR and senior management to decide.

Here is a good reminder of the most important rule in this book: when faced with a difficult situation with an employee, or when you encounter a red flag, bring it to HR's attention immediately.

I anticipate that in the years to come, as society becomes more accepting and generally more aware of transgender and nonbinary individuals, issues around workplace accommodations will become more prevalent. At the same time, employment litigators will see an uptick in lawsuits brought by transgender applicants and employees. Hopefully, you and the organization you lead will enact policies and practices to provide appropriate and respectful accommodations for transgender individuals.

Topic 7: If an Applicant Confirms They Can Legally Work in the United States, Avoid Discussing the Applicant's Citizenship and National Origin

This is another easy one to follow. Provided an applicant has confirmed in their application that they can legally work in the United States, the issue of citizenship and national origin should not come up during a job interview. I have seen companies get into hot water when, in an effort to be friendly and strike up small talk, hiring managers ask applicants where they were born, comment on an applicant's accent, or ask why the applicant decided to immigrate to the United States. While these questions are unlikely to result in a discrimination claim, they are unnecessary. To be clear, unambiguously discriminatory comments or questions, such as "We prefer to only hire Americans," or "Being that you are a foreigner, do you think you can relate to our customers' way of life?" are way out of bounds. The only time an applicant's citizenship *may* be discussed at a job interview is when the position involves issues of national security, and the federal government has specific requirements concerning certain employees' citizenship status. If your company is required to make a citizenship determination for its employees, you already know what I am talking about. For the vast majority of individuals who do not work in national security–type positions, you should stay away from any questions that even remotely touch upon the applicant's national origin and citizenship once the they confirm their right to work in the United States.

Topic 8: Check with HR before Asking Any Questions about an Applicant's Salary History

Historically, an employee's salary history has been a significant factor—if not the most important one—in setting their new pay. The problem with basing compensation at a new job on past compensation is that when one group has historically been paid less than another, this pattern can result in significant pay disparities over time. Of course, the group I am referring to is women.

In 2019, before the pandemic, the national median annual pay for a woman working full-time was $41,977, while the median annual pay for a man working full-time was $52,146. This translates to the often-cited statistic that women in the United States are paid approximately 80 cents for every one dollar paid to men, amounting to an annual gender wage gap of $10,169.[1] Aggregated across the country, women employed full time in the United States are *underpaid* by more than $900 billion every year as a result of the gender pay gap.[2] There are a slew of local, state, and federal laws addressing pay inequality, including laws covering gender, race, and national origin. In many instances, compliance with these laws typically falls on the shoulders of boards of directors and CEOs (i.e., well above the pay grade [pun certainly intended] of most frontline managers). One significant area where frontline managers play an important role in closing the pay gap, however, involves the questions the hiring manager asks during the job interview.

There currently is no federal standard as to what categories of information related to pay equity must be avoided. Many states and cities, however, have adopted strict rules regarding what type of information can be asked during a job interview. It is very important that you familiarize yourself with your company's policies and the law(s) that govern this issue in your city or state. I anticipate that within the next decade, the federal government will set a national standard on the categories of information employers can obtain during the interview stage around the issue of compensation. Until then, leaders need to tread lightly in this area.

Topic 9: Be Careful about Questions Concerning an Applicant's Criminal Record

You have likely heard the phrase "ban-the-box" in the context of background checks and job interviews. The "box" this refers to concerns questions on a job application about whether or not a candidate has been convicted of a crime. The "ban the box" movement started in the late 1990s but really picked up steam during the Great Recession of 2007–2009. The movement is based on the notion that many otherwise qualified individuals are being disproportionally shut out of the job market because they have a past criminal record.

Proponents of the movement cite two main factors for why employers should not inquire about criminal histories before making a job offer. First, with decreased employment opportunities, ex-convicts are more likely to commit crimes. To lower the recidivism rate (committing new crimes and ending up back in prison), which is a benefit to both the individual and society at large, we need to do a much better job reintegrating these folks. And second, certain minority groups and poor people in general are disproportionally entangled in the criminal justice system, often for nonviolent drug charges.

While this movement has for the most part been bipartisan, it certainly has its share of detractors. Some feel that employers should be able to decide whether to favor law-abiding applicants over those with criminal records. Others have cited the law of unintended consequences. As we will discuss in the next chapter, the destructive power of bias has unfortunately prompted some employers who are not permitted to ask about criminal records to use an applicant's race or ethnicity as a proxy for criminal history. This leads to a whole separate problem of race discrimination.[3]

Public policy arguments aside, a growing number of states and cities have imposed restrictions on the information companies can obtain on the subject of criminal histories. Hiring managers must be conversant in the laws that govern the city and state where they are hiring employees. Take California's version of the Ban-the-Box law, for example, known as the Fair

Chance Act. The law bars most employers from asking questions about a candidate's conviction history before making a job offer. If the employer conducts a criminal background check after the conditional job offer has been made, and wants to rescind the offer, the employer also must perform an individualized assessment articulating why the nature and gravity of the prior criminal history precludes the individual from working in that job. Whereas a recent conviction for criminal elder abuse could bar an individual from working at a senior care facility, a 10-year-old conviction for drug possession would not typically bar someone from working at a bakery. California further requires that the employer notify the individual in writing of its decision to rescind the job offer and give the individual five business days to respond to the preliminary decision. The employer then must consider the supplemental evidence provided by the employee and issue a final decision in writing. In other words, the employer must engage in an interactive process with the potential employee before deciding to rescind a job offer. While employers in most other states are not held to the same high standard as California employers, I anticipate more jurisdictions will adopt similarly stringent laws over the next decade, particularly as more and more drug offenses are decriminalized. Again, remember the mantra: when in doubt, seek advice from HR.

Topic 10: Tread Lightly Regarding Questions Concerning an Applicant's Mental or Physical Disabilities

During the interview stage, a hiring manager may ask questions confirming that the applicant can perform the essential functions of the position. If the applicant presents themselves with a physical or mental disability or discloses that they have one, it is generally acceptable to ask the applicant to describe how they will perform essential job duties with or without reasonable accommodations. This line of questions should be limited in scope, and the employer should generally accept what the applicant says during the interview as true. It is wise to inform the applicant of the employer's EEO policy and that the employer is committed to abiding by its legal obligations with respect to accommodating disabled applicants and employees. Further confirmation that the employee can safely perform the essential job duties with or without reasonable accommodations can be required post-offer but before the employee starts working. Actions to determine that the employee is "fit" to perform the position are generally legal as long as (1) the medical examination is job-related, (2) the examination is consistent with a business necessity, and (3) *all* new employees in that job classification are required to undergo the same examination. As a best practice, any questions concerning the accommodation of a disabled applicant and/or employee should be brought to HR's attention to ensure a proper interactive process.

SELECTION TIME

Consider the following scenario. You have finished interviewing five candidates and are ready to make an offer. Of the five you interviewed, one clearly had neither the experience nor the ability to do the job and should never have gotten past the phone screen. The second had the experience but showed very little interest in the position. You have the strong sense that the candidate only applied as leverage to use in salary negotiations with their current employer. That leaves three strong candidates. As the hiring manager, the choice rests with you. At this point, two questions emerge: (1) How do you lawfully choose the best candidate and properly document your decision? and (2) What, if anything, should you say to the candidates that did not get the job—in particular, the two strong applicants?

Lawfully Choosing the Right Candidate

Making hiring decisions is not a paint-by-numbers exercise. When deciding whom to hire, leaders are expected to harness their skills and experience and use considerable discretion. Provided the recruiting and interviewing phases are legally compliant, and as long as the hiring manager does not interject unlawful discriminatory factors, the final result should be entirely clean and above-board (i.e., the best candidate is selected in compliance with the employer's EEO policy). Remember your fourth-grade math teacher who gave you only partial credit for getting the right answer because you failed to "show your work"? Managers should also show their work. When making hiring decisions, managers should document how and why they reached their ultimate decision as a best practice.

There are three primary methods managers tend to use when making hiring decisions. The first method, referred to as the "Scoring Method," has the look and feel of an objective analysis. Employers who use the Scoring Method create a chart or spreadsheet and assign a numerical value to different categories, often on a 1–5 scale. This method identifies strengths and weakness based on specific categories. Some employers go one step further and assign weights to each category. Common fields using the Scoring Method are (a) education, (b) prior work experience, (c) verbal communication, (d) written communication, (e) demonstration of grit, (f) interpersonal skills, (g) problem solving, (h) understanding of industry, (i) knowledge of company, and (j) overall recommendations. This method *can* do a decent job removing implicit bias from the interview process by focusing on the hard and soft skills that a strong employee will have.

The second common method managers use to rank candidates is the "Narrative Method." Rather than assigning a specific number or ranking, the narrative method has the interviewer answer specific questions directly related to core competencies or other factors the employer uses in choosing a new hire. The advantage of the Narrative Method is that it forces hiring managers to think critically in response to every question rather than just jot down numbers. The disadvantage is that it tends to be more time consuming.

The third approach is a classic hybrid, where hiring managers rate candidates using a numerical scale, while noting limited narrative responses. For companies that utilize applicant evaluation forms, this is the most common method.

Regardless of the format in place, every hiring manager should be mindful of the language they use when discussing candidates. In addition to avoiding words that could be seen as offensive or discriminatory, it is important to demonstrate that throughout the hiring process the manager applied the same standards when interviewing every candidate. Consider a hiring manager who spends most of the interviews with male applicants discussing football, yet grills the female applicants about their industry knowledge. It would be difficult for the hiring manager to show why he hired the male candidate over the female candidate—even if that was ultimately the right choice.

Ultimately the act of putting pen to paper is particularly useful in justifying why a manager selected one applicant over the other. It has the added benefit of showing the hiring manager's boss that the manager takes hiring decisions seriously and professionally. Documenting the decision-making process also provides cover should things go south. If you hire enough employees over the years, you will most certainly have a stack of ex-employees who did not work out, including some who were awful hires. Documenting why you hired the individual in the first place is particularly helpful in the event the applicant who did not make the final cut files a discrimination lawsuit. The law does not require leaders to make the best decisions when it comes to hiring and firing, but it does require that employers avoid illegal factors in the interview process.

Effectively Communicating with Individuals Who Did Not Get the Job

Most companies have their own specific protocols about what to say and not say when communicating with a candidate who did not get a job. Many companies send written rejection letters (often via email) when someone applies for a position but does not advance to the interview stage. Some other companies do not send any communication letting the applicant know that they are not being considered for a job. The application just falls into an abyss. The same goes for applicants who spend time preparing for and partic-ipating in a job interview. Some hiring managers or HR partners call every applicant to decline them, while others send a brief email or letter. Still other hiring managers do not communicate the decision at all to the candidate.

If your company leaves it up to you as to what and how to communicate to applicants who do not get a job offer, I have a few suggestions. First, be gracious. Thank the person for applying while letting them know that the company has selected another candidate (or is continuing to interview other applicants). Second, do not tell the candidate the name of the person who ultimately got the job (applicable only to external hires). Third, if a candi-dates asks you why they were not hired, you can (a) tell them that as a policy the company does not provide feedback when someone does not get a job (as long as that is in fact the organization's policy, or at least your policy); (b) in a few sentences, tell the candidate the highlights of why you hired someone else (e.g., other candidates had more experience with X or Y); or (c) depending on how comfortable you are with the applicant, provide constructive criticism so that the candidate has a better understanding of their areas of opportunity. And finally, if you liked the candidate and would consider them in the future, let them know that if opportunities open up, they are encouraged to reapply.

...

Now that we have covered the interview and hiring process, we will explore how to make hiring and employment decisions without falling into the implicit bias trap.

MANAGING WITHOUT FEAR PLAYBOOK

Ten Topics to Avoid When Interviewing a Job Applicant

1. Whether the applicant has children or intends to have children.
2. The applicant's age.
3. The applicant's religion. Also, never assume that the employer will not be able to accommodate a candidate's religious needs based on how the candidate looks.
4. Politics.
5. The reason why a military veteran left the military.
6. The applicant's sexuality and gender identity.
7. Other than confirming that the applicant can legally work in the United States, avoid discussing the applicant's citizenship and national origin.
8. Unless HR approves it, avoid questions about the applicant's salary history.
9. Check with HR before asking a candidate a question about their criminal record.
10. Tread very lightly regarding questions concerning an applicant's mental or physical disabilities.

CHAPTER 5

The Implicit Bias Conundrum

How to Acknowledge, Uncover, and Destroy Implicit Bias in the Workplace

If I may be so presumptuous, allow me to make two assumptions about you.

Assumption Number One:

> You are *not* a racist, bigot, or chauvinist. You do not believe that a person's intelligence, abilities, and value in society are determined by their race, ethnicity, gender, sexual orientation, or religion. You do not subscribe to a supremacist worldview that one group (i.e., white people, men, straight people, etc.) are inherently better than those not in that group. You get the point. I assume that as a leader you do not intentionally make personnel decisions based on discriminatory beliefs or animus toward a particular group.

Assumption Number Two:

> You, like everyone, harbor *some* implicit biases. Throughout your life you have been exposed to millions of experiences, images, and media. When combined in the neuron soup of your brain, they have etched certain stereotypes into your

subconscious. Like everyone else, your life experiences have created a repository of stereotypes—the oversimplified generalizations, both positive and negative, about a person or group of people without regard to a person's individual differences—which, as we will discuss below, *can* impact everyday decisions, including workplace decisions. To be clear, just because you (like me and everyone else who occupies this little blue planet) have implicit biases somewhere in the recesses of your subconscious, it certainly does not in any way mean or imply that you are a racist or bigot. It merely means that you—again, like everyone else—can benefit from employing a handful of strategies to debug your decision-making processes.

Nearly 2,500 years ago, Greek philosopher Plato proposed that everything in the physical world is merely an effort by the designer to copy images of the "ideal"—referred to as Plato's Theory of Forms. The classic example is a chair. Plato believed that every person has the same image of the perfect "chair" in their mind that we use to judge all other chairs. For example, if you are shopping for a chair at IKEA, you have a vision for what the ideal chair looks like in your head. You use that ideal when deciding which chair to purchase. Today, Plato's philosophy that everything in the world is merely an attempt to copy an ideal form is rather silly. There is no such thing as a perfect or ideal house, car, shirt, chair, or person. Perhaps, unknowingly, Plato's Theory of Forms was an effort on his part to make sense of how the subconscious organizes information in our brains and unwittingly promotes implicit bias and stereotypes. That is, Plato mistook the sheer power of the subconscious as somehow creating an ideal in the cosmos, failing to recognize that because no two people share the same subconscious, there can be no single ideal form.

Fast forward two millennia to the 1970s, where famed psychologists Amos Tversky and Daniel Kahneman (the founders of behavioral economics) began studying the impact of the subconscious on what psychologists had previously considered to be "rational" decision making. They examined the impact of heuristics, or mental shortcuts, on how people make decisions without complete information. Heuristics are the patterns and generalizations that help us make decisions using intuitive judgment, common sense, and our "gut feeling." Mental shortcuts are invaluable in our day-to-day lives in that they allow us to make quick decisions. However, as Professors Tversky and Kahneman revealed, heuristics can unwittingly lead to decisions clouded by stereotypes and bias if left unchecked.

In his book *Strangers to Ourselves: Discovering the Adaptive Unconscious*, Professor Timothy Wilson of the University of Virginia writes that the human brain processes 11 million bits of information per second via the five senses (the eye alone processes 10 million bits of information per second). However, of these roughly 11 million pieces of information that shape how we interact with the world around us every second, we consciously process only 40 pieces of information at most. This means that we absorb billions of pieces of information that bypass our conscious mind and build overlapping webs of patterns in our subconscious minds. The study of heuristics helps explain how the information stored in our subconscious directly impacts our decision-making processes.

Think about the last time you went out for dinner at a restaurant. Did you spend hours scrutinizing the menu, carefully considering the tastes, health benefits, environmental ramifications, and costs of each ingredient in each item on the menu, eventually arriving at an decision? No, you likely spent less than a minute looking over the menu before you decided what you wanted to eat. You were able to make this decision, knowing full well that you did not consider all of the pertinent information available, because you used your heuristics to streamline the ordering process. It is frankly more efficient to use heuristics than to deliberate for hours. We tend to use the same decision-making process when we decide which television programs to binge-watch or which books to read. We make decisions based on what we have liked and disliked in the past, and use what our gut tells us to chart our next course of action. We are conditioned to place the utmost faith in the power of our subconscious. We use it as a tool to keep us safe (the subconscious directs the fight vs. flight reaction), to help us decide between an array of options (why having a "gut" feeling about a decision tends to be the most important driver), and even rely on it to find love.

The problem with our overreliance on heuristics is that by definition the subconscious is a compilation of experiences, feelings, and impressions that began forming in our infant brains. It is especially difficult to weed out those aspects of our subconscious that, like a computer virus infecting a piece of software, contain negative stereotypes, impressions, and biases. Implicit bias inevitably seeps into the unconscious (or as NPR journalist and author Shankar Vedantam refers to it, our "hidden brain"). Fortunately, once a person is aware that biases exist, there are several practical steps they can take to de-bias their decisions and actions (like Marie Kondo's home decluttering philosophy for the subconscious).

Before we discuss the debugging process, it is first important to engage in a handful of experiments. For these experiments to work, please read the following three scenarios and honestly answer all of the questions after each scenario based on your initial thoughts, perceptions, and snap judgments. Do not answer the questions based on what is politically correct or how you would answer it if a human resources manager were looking over your shoulder. The only way to declutter implicit bias is by being able to identify it in the first place.

Scenario One: "Congratulations, I'm Having A Baby!"

You are the vice president of finance at your company. You supervise two employees, Charles and Rachelle. Charles, who has been with the company for 10 years, is a decent performer. He's not exceptional, but he's a solid individual contributor. Rachelle is a superstar. She has been with the company for three years and will be up for a considerable promotion in the next few months. Charles is a good team player but Rachelle is essential to the success of your team. Your company is in the process of completing a major acquisition which will significantly increase your team's workload beginning in June.

On Monday morning, Charles comes into your office to share his good news. He and his wife are expecting their second child. You recall that when his first child was born, he took four weeks of paternity leave, and then returned full time. While he was tired and a bit scattered for the first few weeks after returning from leave, he quickly got into his old routine. On Wednesday, Rachelle comes to you with her own good news. Smiling from ear to ear, Rachelle, who is not married, tells you that she is expecting her first child. Coincidently, both Rachelle and Charles's wife are due on June 3rd—smack dab in the middle of your company's major acquisition.

As the manager in this scenario, please honestly answer the following questions based on your actual thoughts, not how you think you *should* respond:

- What are the first three words that come to mind when you heard Charles's news? Do the same exercise when thinking about Rachelle's news.
- How do you personally feel about Rachelle's news that she is expecting a baby? Does her news impact, even slightly, how you view her future with your team or her chances of promotion?
- Did you react any differently when you heard the news that Charles's wife is pregnant compared to when Rachelle told you about her pregnancy?
- Do you have concerns with how Rachelle's venture into motherhood will impact you and your team? Do you have similar concerns about Charles's second child?
- You really want to ask Rachelle how long she plans on being on leave and whether she intends to return full-time or part-time. Are these questions permissible?

Scenario Two: "Ummm, Nice to Meet You…"

You are vice president of talent acquisition for a growing e-commerce company. For the past five months, you have been recruiting for a new IT manager to lead a 10-person, rapidly growing team. After several rounds of phone interviews with a handful of qualified candidates, you are thrilled to have found Monica. Both on paper and over the phone, she is everything you dreamed of in an IT Manager: smart, practical, solution-oriented, and a demonstrated leader. The final interview is more of a "get-to-know-you" than a formal interview. In your mind, unless Monica completely botches it, the position is hers. Monica arrives at the interview and you immediately notice that she is obese. The picture you had of Monica in your mind, based on her outdated LinkedIn profile, is very different from the person who walks into your office.

Honestly answer the following questions based on your snap judgment:

- What is your initial feeling when you see that Monica is significantly overweight?
- Are you disappointed?
- Does Monica's weight in any way change your perception of her as a leader?
- Would you feel the same if, instead of Monica, the final candidate is Tim, a man who also happens to be overweight?
- Do you have negative feelings about people who are overweight?

Scenario Three: Ivy League vs. Mini-Me

You are a successful male business consultant and a partner in your management consulting company. You need to hire a junior analyst for your growing team. You are deciding between two candidates, both in their final semesters of college. Whoever you ultimately hire will immediately become your mentee. You will be expected to train this new employee, nurture their growth, and if all goes well, after many years working together in the trenches, you will be in a position to advocate for your mentee to become a partner in the firm. You will end up spending a considerable amount of time with the candidate you select, including countless weeks on the road working on projects for your clients.

The first candidate, Maria, is about to graduate with honors from an Ivy League college—where she received a full scholarship. For the last three years, she has worked 25 hours a week as a math tutor and in the college library. She is president of the school's Latinx business club. In addition to English, Maria speaks Spanish and Portuguese, which could be very helpful for your growing Latin American business. Maria grew up poor. She helped raise her two younger siblings while her parents worked multiple low-paying jobs to provide for their family. You are very impressed with Maria. Yet, although you would never verbalize it to anyone, it's clear that you and Maria do not have much in common. You respect Maria's intelligence and work ethic, but you are concerned that it will be difficult to "connect" with her given your different interests and life experiences.

The second candidate, Greg, will graduate with a 3.2 GPA from a mid-tier college, which happens to be your alma mater. Greg is the social chair of his fraternity, which happens to be your old fraternity (making him your "brother"). Greg volunteers once a month teaching golf to inner-city children. He has not needed to work while in college, as he has been fortunate to rely on his parents for financial support. Greg grew up in an upper-middle class family. His father is an accountant and his mother is a middle school principal. Greg is very outgoing and personable. Although he only speaks English, he tells you that he will use his charm and "savvy business mind" (he is dripping with confidence) when working with your Latin American clients. You first met Greg at the annual fraternity alumni football game and immediately hit it off. You have very similar interests. You are both avid golfers, hold similar political beliefs, and like the same movies. Your colleagues are already referring to Greg as your "mini-me."

Please honestly answer the following questions, putting yourself in the shoes of the white male hiring manager deciding between Maria and Greg:

- Which candidate is your gut telling you to hire? Why?
- Which candidate is your brain telling you that you *should* hire?
- How are you going to make your decision?
- If you are leaning toward Greg, what about him appeals to you as compared to Maria?
- Are you concerned that Maria, while clearly qualified and exceptional, will not be the right "fit" for what you are looking for? What does it mean to be the right fit?
- Does each applicant's gender, class, and/or ethnicity impact your decision?

Let's unpack each of the scenarios so you can check my earlier hypothesis that implicit bias not only exists (a matter that should not be up for debate), but can be particularly problematic in the employment context.

Reviewing Scenario One: "Congratulations, I'm Having a Baby!"

In the first scenario, we learned about Charles and Rachelle. Recall that Charles told you his wife is expecting her second child, and Rachelle told you she is expecting her first, as a single mother. Did you react differently to their news? Did you have concerns that when she comes back to work after maternity leave, Rachelle will lack the same drive and dedication she had before she became a mother?

You no doubt have concluded that the Charles/Rachelle scenario is intended to elicit the perils of gender discrimination. Of course the manager in this scenario, like all three scenarios, has yet to do anything wrong. What the manager does or does not do next and the reasons—implicit and explicit—for these decisions will either serve to propagate or eliminate bias.

At its most basic level, holding Charles and Rachelle to different standards because of their gender is discriminatory. That is obvious. However, a careful reader will point out that the manager in this scenario has consistently treated Charles and Rachelle equally and has not done anything that would suggest the manager engages in gender discrimination. Case in point, the manager considers Rachelle a "superstar" on the fast-track for promotion, while Charles is seen as an average performer. So why raise the alarm now? Why do the manager's feelings and gut reactions matter? Don't actions, not thoughts, dictate how we are evaluated at work? Why have this discussion at all? The answer to these questions is because if the manager in our scenario does not pause to reflect on the situation, the manager's bias could lead to the manager making a decision that violates the company's own equal opportunity policies and the law.

Reviewing Scenario Two: "Ummm, Nice to Meet You..."

The second scenario identifies the well-documented biases overweight people, and especially overweight women, often face in the workplace. In their research on the prevalence of discrimination against overweight people, Professors Emma Levine of the University of Chicago and Maurice Schweitzer of the University of Pennsylvania found that obese people are widely discriminated against in the workplace, and across the board are perceived to be of low competence.[1] In other words, there is a pernicious stereotype that overweight people are not as competent, and therefore not as valuable, in the workplace.

A study by the Centers for Disease Control and Prevention found that obese people receive lower starting salaries, tend to be ranked as less qualified, and are required to work longer hours compared to employees of normal weight.[2] Researchers at Southern Illinois University found that obese women are much more likely to be discriminated against than obese men when applying for a job, particularly in high-profile jobs.[3]

Getting back to Monica. When the manager in our case study first met Monica in person, the manager's gut feeling raised a concern because of Monica's weight. If the manager does not immediately check her bias, her gut feeling (based on a lifetime of negative thoughts and associations about overweight people) could result in Monica not getting a job she is clearly qualified for. Of course, if the manager checks her bias and recognizes that it would be entirely unfair (and in some jurisdictions illegal) to discriminate against Monica because of her weight, Monica would get the job based on her experiences, talents, and proven success.

Reviewing Scenario Three: Ivy League versus Mini-Me

Where the first scenario identifies the specific dangers associated with implicit gender bias, and the second focused on implicit bias toward overweight people, the third scenario touches upon two of the biggest culprits of implicit bias in the workplace: affinity bias and the halo effect.

Affinity bias is the tendency to give preference to people like us, and in so doing place a thumb on the scale in favor of those who look like us, come from a similar socioeconomic backgrounds, or have a shared cultural experience. The halo effect is often paired with affinity bias. If we are predisposed to favoring certain people because we naturally gravitate toward those whom we have an "affinity" towards, we tend to justify our reasons by focusing on one attribute the individual has (and typically other comparators lack). This becomes a "halo" over the person we favor, which has undue influence over our perceptions about that person.

Let us examine our third scenario. By virtually every objective metric (academic achievement, work ethic, languages spoken, grit, etc.), Maria is a much stronger candidate than Greg. However, her future as a successful consultant with the company may never come to fruition if the hiring manager fails to check his bias before making the hiring decision. First, the manager will need to call attention to the often-overwhelming allure of affinity bias. He clearly likes Greg (his fraternity brother) on a personal level and sees much of himself in Greg. And while chemistry between a manager and a subordinate is certainly important, placing *too* much emphasis on interpersonal chemistry over other important attributes leads to "bias creep."

Second, if the manager offers the position to Greg over Maria because he believes Greg is "more social" and will do a better job "connecting" with clients, he will be falling into the halo effect trap. There is an inherent problem with a determination that Greg will be a better junior analyst because he appears to be more charismatic than Maria: a belief that may be the result of gender and cultural biases. This single attribute—even if it were true and legitimate—serves as a halo, covering up Greg's other shortcomings compared to Maria. If the hiring manager bases his decision primarily on this one factor, he is allowing one attribute to overshadow other attributes, likely because it is one area where Greg *appears* to be stronger than Maria.

The third area of concern in the Greg/Maria scenario comes down to the hiring manager putting his heuristics on autopilot. The manager's gut feeling that Greg is a better fit for the position is by all accounts not based on any objective measures, but rather on what is perceived to be Greg's "intangibles." It is certainly reasonable for the hiring manager to consult with what his gut feelings are telling him about this decision. He needs to recognize that his gut feelings are not always reliable, however, and that following his gut over other significant factors can lead directly to discrimination.

DECLUTTERING IMPLICIT BIAS

There is a healthy debate in the scientific community as to whether the human brain is capable of altering unconscious thoughts and biases. One school of thought takes the position that implicit attitudes are activated without us even knowing they exist, and that they are essentially immutable. Scholars in this camp argue that implicit attitudes are learned at a very early age and are then reinforced throughout childhood, adolescence, and into adulthood. They argue that by the time a fully formed adult brain sets out to make decisions that touch upon such biases, they cannot be changed. The only way to solve this problem then, is by educating parents and teachers about how stereotypes and biases burrow into the developing brain, so that they can educate children from an early age to avoid incorporating bias into their subconscious.

The second school of thought argues that while implicit biases are extremely difficult to unlearn, there are specific strategies adults can incorporate into their thought processes when making decisions that can refashion heuristics, and in the process debug the subconscious. This school of thought believes that with enough attention and self-awareness, implicit attitudes are malleable.

I am a proponent of the malleability theory. I certainly acknowledge the mountains of scientific literature establishing that implicit biases are so deeply implanted in the hardware of our operating systems that when pressed to make a split-second decision it is nearly impossible to correct for our biases. I believe that with enough training, however, the human brain is able to remove, or at the very least call attention to and decrease, implicit bias when making deliberate decisions. This is particularly true in the workplace. In other areas of our lives, we have the absolute freedom in the United States to rely on our heuristics when, for example, choosing our friends, adopting a political philosophy, and deciding which movies to watch. In the workplace, however, we have a legal obligation to make decisions that do not discriminate against those in protected classifications.

Dr. Nilanjana Dasgupta, professor of psychology at the University of Massachusetts-Amherst and founder of the Implicit Social Cognition Lab, has written extensively on practical measures people can adopt to help remove implicit bias from the decision-making process. Let us focus on a few of the concrete strategies Dr. Dasgupta and other researchers have developed to combat implicit bias in the workplace.

Strategy One: Educate Yourself

Several studies have shown that people are in a better position to make decisions clear of implicit bias simply by knowing how implicit bias works and the dangers associated with bias creep.[4] The good news here is that the very act of reading this chapter puts you in a much better position to spot and react to implicit bias. But awareness of this issue does not end the discussion; it merely starts it.

Strategy Two: Be Motivated to Suppress Stereotypes and Negative Thoughts

Identifying and reacting to implicit bias is a difficult undertaking for everyone. This is especially true for managers tasked with implementing policies that conflict with implicit biases they held based on social norms and closely held religious beliefs. It is difficult, but not impossible. I learned this lesson several years ago after giving a lecture on employment law to regional managers of a large global company. At the end of the lecture, I was approached by one of the attendees (we will call him Jim), who shared the following story.

Jim started by telling me that he loved his job and his team of 55 sales employees spread across Florida, Georgia, Alabama, Mississippi, and Louisiana. He had worked for his company for 10 years, and planned on retiring in four years when he turned 67. Jim told me that before starting with this company, he was a pastor at a mid-sized church outside of Mobile, Alabama. While he cherished his role as a religious leader, he decided to leave the clergy and pursue a job in sales so he could make more money to support his growing family. Although he stepped down from a paid position with his church, he continued to serve as a community leader, teaching Sunday School and leading missions to South America every summer.

Jim told me that about a decade ago, his company revised its national antidiscrimination policy to include protecting gay and lesbian applicants and employees, even though the states where *he* worked did not treat homosexuality as a protected class (this conversation took place before the Supreme Court's 2020 ruling in *Bostock v. Clayton County, Georgia* that included homosexuality as a protected class under federal antidiscrimination laws, as discussed in Chapter 10). He shared that while he understood why the company expanded the list of individuals protected by the EEO policy, he struggled with how to implement the new policy. He made it clear that while he has no reason to believe he ever intentionally discriminated against gays and lesbians at work, he was nevertheless concerned that the work culture in his region was not especially inclusive when it came to sexual orientation. Jim also mentioned he grew up with rather negative views and stereotypes toward gay people. Based on his religious upbringing, where he learned from a young age that homosexuality is a sin, he held personal biases toward LGBTQ+ folks.

Faced with this dilemma—abiding by company policy while reconciling his personal beliefs and explicit and implicit biases—he reached out to his HR business partner for advice. Unfortunately, his HR contact's only advice was that he had to abide by the new policy and figure it out himself. Beyond that, the HR manager did not offer any recommendations on how Jim could overcome his biases.

At that point, Jim had two options. He could have given lip service to the new policy by acknowledging it but doing little if anything to overcome his personal biases and create a truly inclusive workplace. He could, on the other hand, have taken active measures to address his biases and fears about homosexuality, with the goal of getting to a place where he could be a leader who welcomed and supported all of his employees, regardless of sexual orientation. He chose the latter.

Jim described the steps he took to debug his decision making. He decided that before he had conversations with his team members about this new policy, he needed to better understand LGBTQ+ culture. Remember that up to that point he only had negative associations about LGBTQ+ folks. He began reading up on the LGBTQ+ experience in America. He also visited the library of a nearby university and found studies about how gay men in particularly have been discriminated against in the United States, and how anti-gay slurs (slurs he would never use but has certainly heard) can lead to a hostile work environment. Because he told me that he had no gay friends or acquaintances at the time (and if he did they were in the closet), he arranged to speak with a friend's brother who was a gay man living in a nearby city. He recalls the conversation as "eye opening." He heard about how challenging it was for this gay man to be out in the community but closeted at work and his constant fear that he could be fired from his job simply because of his sexuality.

After a few months of coming to terms with his own prejudices, Jim set aside two hours at a regional team meeting to train his colleagues on how to create a more inclusive environment for LGBTQ+ employees. He recalled that a week after this meeting, he met with one of his top performing employees for a one-on-one training session. During the meeting, she broke down in tears, telling Jim that she had been in the closet at work for years. She had been afraid that her coworkers would not understand, or worse, would be hostile if they learned about her sexuality. But after the meeting and hearing about Jim's personal journey, she felt comfortable telling her coworkers about this important part of her life. She even decided to bring her longtime domestic partner to the holiday party that year (this was before gay marriage became legal across the United States in 2015).

I asked Jim if it was still challenging for him to reconcile his personal religious beliefs and implicit biases with his goal of creating an inclusive and accepting work environment. He admitted that it was still difficult, but that he has made considerable strides over the years. He joked that while he has no plans to march in a gay pride parade and continues to see heterosexuality as a biblical mandate, he is a strong advocate for equality when it comes to the workplace.

Jim's story inspired other leaders, as well as nonmanagerial employees within his organization, to address their own personal biases. His intentionality when addressing ways to address his personal biases toward the LGBTQ+ community is admirable. So too is the fact that he sees this as a work in progress, cognizant of the reality that many feelings and stereotypes are so deeply ingrained that it takes constant effort and perseverance to keep them in check.

Strategy Three: Examine Thoughts for Potential Implicit Bias

To avoid falling into an implicit bias trap, one needs enough self-awareness to be able to see the hidden dangers in the first place. An essential tool in being able to debug the decision-making process is having enough metacognition to understand how your personal life experiences and biases impact your gut reactions, and then how your gut feelings can play a supersized role when making decisions.

In the first scenario, we discussed a manager who learned that two key employees on the team were having a baby at the same time. The only difference was that for one employee, his wife was to give birth, and for the other employee, she was the one giving birth. Let's assume that the manager had an implicit bias toward women who intentionally become single mothers. Perhaps the manager was raised by an abusive single mother or has an acrimonious relationship with a family member who chose to have a baby outside of marriage. If this were the case, the manager's gut reaction might have led to a different response to Rachelle's news as compared to Charles's, potentially leading to unequal treatment. Let's further assume that the manager "owned" their hang-ups on this issue and approached any decisions mindful of these biases and ready to have a rational discussion. Once able to recognize the existence of implicit bias, the manager could feel more confident in whatever decision they made when preparing for two key employees to be on a leave of absence at the same time.

Strategy Four: Avoid Distracted or Pressured Decision Making

As a leader, you are constantly bombarded with high-pressure situations. All too often you have to quickly make personnel decisions—whether it be staffing, recommendations for promotions, or assigning blame—in a chaotic environment without enough time. And while a strong leader is able to make good decisions in a high-pressure environment, having time to deliberate is an imperative with sensitive personnel decisions. One of the goals of this book is to help leaders slow down the process when making personnel decisions. While this lesson is important in all areas of employee management, it is particularly acute when working to remove the impact of implicit bias.

Strategy Five: Be Willing to Engage in Intergroup Contact

Perhaps the best way to truly break down implicit biases, stereotypes, and negative associations is by getting to know people who, by birth, choice, or life circumstances, are part of stigmatized groups. There is considerable evidence that more contact with counter-stereotypes, including having meaningful interactions in the workplace, is an effective way to combat implicit bias.[5] Jim's decision to learn firsthand about the challenges gay men face in corporate America, and how that experience reshaped his own attitudes, is but one example of the force of intergroup contact.

This strategy applies in the absence of negative biases toward certain groups. In this chapter's third scenario, you were asked to stand in the shoes of the male manager who had to decide between two candidates: Maria and Greg. There is no indication in the scenario as presented that the manager harbored any negative associations toward Maria. His reluctance to offer the job to Maria may be partly the result of affinity bias and the halo effect in favor of Greg. It may also reflect a subconscious concern on his part that he might have a difficult time relating to Maria on a personal level due to the significant differences in their backgrounds. If the manager is willing to learn about Maria's culture and life experiences—provided she is open to sharing aspects of her personal life with her manager—this will likely result in breaking down barriers and creating a more inclusive work culture.

Addressing implicit bias, on both a personal level and within the workplace, is a key component to the Managing Without Fear philosophy. Tackling this issue head-on creates a more inclusive and legally compliant workplace. Leaders who heed this advice will also be able to use their knowledge to make more thoughtful and rational decisions that are free from, or at least not overwhelmed by, biased heuristics.

• • • • • • • • • • •
MANAGING WITHOUT FEAR PLAYBOOK

Effective Strategies for Avoiding
Implicit Bias in the Workplace

1. Educate yourself about the science behind implicit bias.
2. Be motivated to suppress stereotypes and negative thoughts when making personnel decisions.
3. Put personnel decisions under the "implicit bias lens."
4. Work to avoid distracted and pressured decision making when making personnel decisions.
5. Be willing to engage in serious intergroup contact and self-reflection.

CHAPTER 6

Making the Most of the First Three Months

The Art of Onboarding a New Hire

PART 1: AN EPIC ONBOARDING FAILURE

She was born in 1954 in a rural Mississippi town to a teenage mother. She spent her childhood and adolescence as a nomad, living in small towns and medium-sized cities across the country. She alternated between living with her loving, yet harsh, grandmother, her overworked and estranged mother, and her absentee father. Her childhood was a rollercoaster. She was the victim of unimaginable sexual abuse and trauma. Despite all of this, however, she persevered. At an early age, teachers saw that she had a gift of telling stories and connecting with people on a personal level. In high school, she was hired by a local radio station to read news reports on the air. After graduating from college on a full scholarship, where she majored in communications, she became the first African American female TV news anchor at Nashville's CBS affiliate.

In 1976, the ABC affiliate in Baltimore hired her to coanchor the evening news. This itself was an amazing feat. Here was a 22-year-old African American woman from rural Mississippi who was now coanchoring a major metropolitan news program. At that time, most Americans religiously watched one of the three nightly news programs. Recognizing an opportunity, the station's general manager (GM) used her unique first name—which at the time people struggled to pronounce—to hype the show before its launch. Before her first broadcast, her face and name were plastered on buses and billboards across the city. She was paired with a much older and more established anchor, who as she only later found out, was upset and likely jealous that a young and charismatic African American woman would be his cohost. The two had zero on-air chemistry. Worse, rather than help her acclimate to the big city and the opportunity to be on the vanguard of the news business (which was particularly unwelcoming to minorities), he went out of his way to frustrate her progress. He belittled her on the air and criticized her for being "too emotional" when reporting on tragedies and human-interest stories. It did not surprise anyone, least of all the young newscaster, that the program that was launched with great fanfare and promise ended up being a complete bust.

On April 1, 1977, the GM called her into his office with bad news. Although she thought it was a cruel April Fool's joke, it was not. The GM took her off of the evening news and relegated her to reading a few minutes of headlines in the morning—one of the lowest and loneliest positions in the newsroom. This was a signal to others that she did not have the chops to "make it" in the news business. Her former cohost got what he wanted. She was blamed for the show's failure, and he kept his seat on the nightly news program.

Her story did not end there, although it certainly could have. Rather than take the rejection, pack her bags, and move back to Nashville to find another way to make a living, she endured and eventually found her way back on the air to host a fledgling talk show. Eventually, that young woman became the most successful female media personality in history and the star of her own nationally syndicated show for 25 years. That woman, of course, is Oprah Winfrey.

This book is not about how successful people overcome life challenges, but rather how leaders can develop the acumen, skills, and courage to manage their employees without fear. So why start a chapter on onboarding new employees discussing Oprah's experience in Baltimore? The reason is simple. While Oprah's achievements are legendary and worthy of close study, I am more concerned with how the GM of the Baltimore station blew the opportunity to work with the "Queen of All Media." How is it that this GM committed one of the worst onboarding *faux pas* in history?

In making this bold hire, the GM clearly had a knack for talent. He saw that Oprah was a natural in front of the camera. So what accounts for his failure? Let's imagine an alternative universe where the GM gave Oprah his full support, fired her male cohost for being a jerk, and helped her achieve her goal of becoming a prominent news anchor. I have no doubt that Oprah would have joined the television news Mount Rushmore of Walter Cronkite, David Brinkley, Peter Jennings, and Diane Sawyer. Although her career as a news anchor did not take off, clearly by any measure of fame, professional success, social impact, and fortune, Oprah is in a league of her own. Yet the question remains, how did her GM let such a talented employee slip through his hands?

Oprah's struggles as cohost of the evening news in Baltimore was not her failure, but that of her manager. Had her manager made a concerted effort to successfully nurture Oprah's professional development during those early days, he would not have squandered the opportunity to work with and mentor the most successful media personality of all time. As we will explore in this chapter, successfully and legally onboarding a new employee is more art than science. Failing to successfully onboard a new employee can lead to a host of serious problems. Effective managers are able to use the onboarding process, and especially the first few months on the job, to set realistic objectives while keying in on any potentially problematic traits and behaviors.

PART 2: MAKING THE MOST OF THE FIRST THREE MONTHS

Unless your organization has a written probationary period for all new employees, I recommend not telling a new hire that they are "on probation" when they first join your team. There is no legally recognized doctrine that new hires must be provided a probationary period. It is a common misconception that after a designated period of time (usually between 3–6 months), a new hire becomes a permanent employee and thereby entitled to greater job protections. And while the concept of a probationary period is not a legal requirement, and typically only exists in unionized workforces, many employees and some managers act as if it is an employee's right. So what should the crucial period when a new employee first joins your team be called? Because onboarding usually lasts a few weeks at most, I suggest swapping out the term "probationary period" and replacing it with the "fusion stage." During the fusion stage, the employee, the leader, and HR work together to integrate the new employee into the organization. For some employees, it may take a few weeks, and for others it may take several months. Either way, at the end of this stage, the manager should know if the employee you just spent considerable time and money hiring is the right fit for your organization.

The fusion stage of the employment relationship consists of five core components: (1) cultural conveyance, (2) skills training, (3) HR policy and procedure education, (4) assessment and feedback, and (5) goal setting and expectation leveling. These objectives are not accomplished sequentially. They are layered, one over the other, until the manager and the employee, often with guidance from HR leaders, are satisfied that the fusion stage is complete.

Many books have been written by management gurus on how to effectively onboard new employees. Some take a philosophical approach, while others offer practical advice on team building. The Managing Without Fear school takes a slightly different view. For managers who want to set the employee up for success while protecting themselves and their employer, the fusion stage establishes the ground rules for the employment relationship going forward. It also gives the manager an opportunity to evaluate their new team member and determine early on whether it is in the organization's best interest to continue to employ this person.

A good friend who is the CEO of a successful life sciences company often tells new employees: "*Here is the deal. We will treat you very well while you are working for this company. However, if the time comes that we decide to end this relationship, we expect you will act professionally, you will not blame anyone else for it not working out, and you will go on to your next adventure. And know now that if you decide to file a frivolous lawsuit against the company, we will never pay you a penny to settle.*" While this message is admittedly a bit harsh, said another way, it is a message that every new employee should want to hear when they start a new job: you will be treated fairly and in accordance with the law, which means that if this job does not work out, you will move on to your next job.

OBJECTIVE ONE: CULTURAL CONVEYANCE

Workplace culture is an amalgam of the organization's core principles, vision, and employment policies and procedures, coupled with the unique personalities of each department, team, and employee. An organization's culture is a binary compound made up of the *internal* culture of its employees combined with the *external* culture (i.e., the organization's reason for existence, or in corporate speak, its "value add" to society). Here we focus primarily on conveying the internal culture to new employees, which, if done well, usually covers the external culture as well.

If you have listened to and read enough management experts discuss workplace culture, as I have, three things become readily apparent. First, there is no working definition of what constitutes workplace culture. Second, there are wildly different views on how organizations "teach" culture to their employees—that is, how it is passed down from the founder to the current CEO/chief visionary, to the leaders, and then to rank-and-file employees. Third, there are passionate disagreements on the virtues of having a so-called "strong" workplace culture with everyone appearing to march to the same drummer versus a more "laid back," decentralized culture that places greater emphasis on the individual contributor. The purpose of *this* book is not to resolve these existential questions. I presume instead that, as a frontline manager, you inherited a workplace culture when you joined your organization. Whatever that culture is, you need to effectively convey this to your new hires.

During the fusion stage, strong leaders must find the time to both teach and model workplace culture. As discussed below, this can be accomplished in several ways. Before we touch upon how to communicate workplace culture to new hires, however, it is important to discuss how *you* feel about your organization's workplace culture.

A leader does not have to be a "cheerleader" for the organization to effectively convey workplace culture. I have represented and trained thousands of frontline managers in virtually every industry. In my survey of the American manager, I have found no correlation between a manager's outward enthusiasm for their employer and their success as a leader. I have come across leaders who are impassioned advocates for their organization. Like a Green

Bay Packers superfan, they wear their company's mission and culture on their sleeves. I have also worked with managers who tend to be much more subdued when it comes to their admiration for their employer. While they fully embrace their organization's mission and take pride in their jobs, they are unlikely to be sent to a job fair to promote their employer. With few exceptions, organizations that demand that their leaders personify the sense of duty, discipline, and purpose a platoon commander has for the Marine Corps will not only be disappointed, but will also fail to attract and keep the best leaders.

It is reasonable, however, for companies to expect that their leaders authentically believe in the organization's mission and vision. For a leader to convey and advocate workplace culture to a new hire, it is helpful if they are able to discuss the organization's culture in personal terms.

Communicating workplace culture is a bit like making a chocolate soufflé. Even if you carefully follow a recipe and meticulously seek out the advice of professional bakers, half the time it comes out inverted and a puddle of chocolate, butter, and sugar. With that in mind, here are a few suggestions:

- It starts, but does not end, with a conversation. Within the first few days of a new hire, a leader who manages without fear should sit down with a new hire and have a candid discussion about the organization's internal and external culture. While this ground was likely covered when the new hire interviewed for the position, it is important to initiate this conversation again, now that the individual joined your team. The difference is that it is no longer a theoretical discussion. The conversation should *not* start with the manager telling the new employee what it is "really like" working for the company, as that reeks of a bait and switch. It should instead be a more in-depth discussion about the organization's core mission and the work culture the organization hopes to foster.
- Tell the organization's story. Having new employees read a letter from the CEO on the first page of the employee handbook or watch an orientation video module on the company's history is not enough. Within a few months on the job, an employee should be able to effectively tell their organization's story. New employees should feel like they are joining a special organization, made up of individuals who share their values, work

ethic, and passion. Once an employee gets a handle on their organization's story, they are able to become a brand ambassador, helping to attract others to become part of the story.

- Make a point to discuss your organization's culture throughout the fusion stage. If you have ever spent a considerable amount of time living abroad, you know that it takes time and effort to assimilate into another culture, and that it cannot be accomplished by reading a guidebook or touring the city's notable tourist spots. As you train the new hire, spend time pointing out how workplace culture and company culture are incorporated into the employees' day-to-day routines. For example, if a key component of a company's culture is environmental stewardship, the training program tailored for new employees should focus on how the organization promotes environmentalism throughout the organization.

A final word of caution about cultural conveyance. Leaders should avoid discussing their organization's culture in a negative manner (e.g., "welcome to hell" or "the pay is decent, but the work is boring"). Nor should they use problematic or illegal phrases to describe the workplace (e.g., "we are a frat culture," or "we are a young and hip workplace," or "we are a company based on traditional Christian values").

OBJECTIVE TWO: SKILLS TRAINING

Training new hires is obviously a cornerstone of the fusion stage. It is so obvious, in fact, that we need not spend time discussing the value of training, nor how to do it properly. One of the reasons you were promoted or hired into leadership is ostensibly because you know how to train your subordinates. There are, however, several themes a leader who manages without fear should be mindful of when training new hires.

Safety is Paramount

According to the federal Occupational Health and Safety Administration (OSHA), the agency responsible for establishing federal health and safety guidelines and regulating employers, inadequate safety training is the leading cause of on-the-job injuries. Workplace health and safety must play a central role during the fusion stage. Managers without fear are confident that their employees know how to safely perform their jobs, know there are significant consequences if they cut corners, and take workplace safety concerns very seriously. If a workplace accident occurs, a manager without fear is able to provide a detailed explanation on how the manager trained the injured employee to prevent the accident. A manager who has properly trained their employees on safety should not be blamed when a subordinate experiences a workplace injury.

Trust and Verify

During interviews, it is not uncommon for candidates to overstate their skills and experiences to land a new job. Several years ago, I represented a company in a sexual orientation discrimination complaint brought by the former chief financial officer (CFO). My client, owner of a technology start-up, hired the employee as its first CFO. The individual aced his interviews. He confidently asserted that he could handle complicated financial transactions. He made the CEO believe that he could walk into the position and immediately take charge of an unruly situation. Within the first few weeks, the other executives found out that their new CFO was woefully unprepared to assume his new role. I wouldn't go so far as to call the ex-employee a con man, but it is a close call. The CEO reviewed her notes from her interviews, and confirmed that the CFO unabashedly overstated his skills and abilities. Taking a page out of the Managing Without Fear toolbox, the CEO took immediate action, called the new employee to task, and shortly thereafter separated his employment. When all of this evidence came to light, the ex-employee's lawyer quickly realized that his client did not have a case and dropped the lawsuit.

The lesson here is that when a new employee is hired, the expectation is that they are coming into the position having already mastered a specific skill or set of skills. During the fusion stage, the manager should trust the new employee's representations, while still verifying that the employee does in fact possess those skills. Just because an employee has overstated their experiences and skills is not necessarily a reason to pull the plug on the relationship. It is imperative, however, that in the first 90 days the manager has a good grasp of the skills the employee has actually mastered to do the job and what skills are still in progress.

Assume the Role of a Teacher, Not a Taskmaster

Schools and universities spend millions of dollars every year on teacher pedagogy—that is, training educators on the most advanced methodologies for teaching students. From formal teacher education and credentialing programs to teacher in-service days, the American educational complex invests considerable time and resources into *how* teachers teach. Educators at every level of the system are expected to incorporate the latest research into their teaching methods. New understandings of brain science and Harvard University professor Howard Gardner's research on multiple intelligences are some examples. Given how much attention we place on pedagogy from nursery school through advanced-level graduate programs, one would assume that the American workforce would similarly focus on how leaders teach their employees. It does not.

Effective leaders approach training opportunities from the perspective of a teacher, not a taskmaster. They apply different modalities to the training process and consider how each employee learns best. While one employee may master a complicated skill by reading a manual, another may learn that same skill by watching the leader do it several times. Still another employee may need to take notes during the training session.

Having a teaching mindset during training does not mean that a leader must coddle their employees. It is simply a recognition that people grasp information in a variety of ways. Having a teaching mindset when training employees results in higher quality output and a more efficient fusion stage. It ultimately makes the manager's job exponentially easier.

Provide Employees a Guide on How to Work with You

New employees are expected to quickly master the organization's culture, policies and procedures, workflows, organization chart, and standard operating procedures. Managers also expect that new employees will become mind readers. It is not uncommon for managers to expect the members of their team to incorporate the manager's idiosyncrasies into their work product.

From relatively minor matters (e.g., how to format documents, where to store supplies, using unique abbreviations, etc.) to more consequential decisions (e.g., the proper tone to use when communicating with a client, when to elevate a sensitive issue up the ladder, etc.), leaders often expect their employees to figure out their style by osmosis.

There is a better way to transfer this knowledge. Managers who have unique demands and expectations of their team members can avoid considerable frustration and reduce their employees' anxiety by issuing their team members a memo entitled "How To Work With Me." To be effective, the memo needs to be grounded in reality. For example, if the leader tends to micromanage their employees, the memo should not shy away from this fact and should describe the decisions the manager must review and/or approve as well as the decisions the team member has discretion over. Writing down one's unique expectations and demands also provides a leader the opportunity to reflect on their own management style. During this process, you may determine that you have certain quirks that are no longer necessary or detract from an efficient workflow.

OBJECTIVE THREE: EDUCATE ON HR POLICIES AND PROCEDURES

There is one question that every defense attorney in an employment case asks a plaintiff (the ex-employee suing their employer) without fail during the plaintiff's deposition: "Did you carefully read the employee handbook that you acknowledged signing when you first started working for the Company?" Having taken hundreds of plaintiffs' depositions, I conservatively estimate that 90 percent of plaintiffs testify that they carefully read the employee handbook. Of the 90 percent who claim that they read and reviewed the entire handbook, based on responses to more specific questions, I estimate that only about 10 percent of them are actually telling the truth.

Employers typically provide their new employees a copy of the employee handbook or their employment policies and have the new employee acknowledge receiving the handbook or policies. Some employers require that new employees take a quiz to confirm they read specific policies. This process is usually overseen by HR during the onboarding process, with little involvement from the new employee's manager.

For leaders who want to fully embrace the Managing Without Fear philosophy, time should be set aside during the fusion stage to review and discuss the organization's employment policies and procedures. I am not suggesting a page-by-page text study, but rather a one-on-one discussion highlighting key policies and procedures. This conversation should at least include a discussion of the organization's policies prohibiting discrimination and harassment, key wage and hour requirements (e.g., prohibition on working off the clock, clocking procedures, etc.), and the different ways employees can address compliance concerns (e.g., the manager, HR, a toll-free complaint number). Such a discussion has the added benefit of sending a clear message to new hires that the manager and organization take compliance seriously. It reinforces the expectation that all employees must similarly embrace a culture of compliance.

OBJECTIVE FOUR: REGULAR ASSESSMENT AND FEEDBACK

A successful fusion stage requires that leaders regularly assess their new employees' skills, abilities, and attitudes. Assessment is integral to the training process, as it gives managers feedback on their employees' progress while providing new employees a better understanding of what skills they still need to master. This is obvious to any successful leader. A manager schooled in the art of managing without fear hopes for the best and plans for the worst. This leader knows that despite everyone's best intentions, there are some new hires that show all the signs that they will be successful contributors and others that, early on, prove to be duds.

The fusion stage gives an attentive manager the opportunity to make what is often a difficult, albeit necessary, decision to separate an employee within a few months of them starting on the job. In my experience, managers tend to be scared of letting an employee go too early in the relationship due to concerns that their decision will not be supported by their boss, HR, and perhaps even the law. And while separating any employee is usually a difficult decision, it is especially complicated when the employee has only been on the team for a few months. A manager without fear is not hamstrung by the foolish notion that every new hire deserves a long runway before deciding to cancel their flight. A manager without fear can demonstrate and document that the employee was treated fairly and legally and was given sufficient time to excel in their new role. They can reference conversations with the new employee where job expectations were discussed and where the manager told the new employee that, absent significant improvement, the organization might have to part ways with the employee.

There are a number of warning signs leaders should be on the lookout during a new hire's first few months on the job. It should be noted that the presence of these warning signs does not necessarily mean that the best course of action is to separate the employee. It does, however, require timely conversations so that the new hire is aware of their deficiencies and understands that their employment could be short-lived without significant improvement.

Warning Sign No. 1

A new employee shows an unwillingness to do the job duties assigned to them, or resists a manager's reasonable instructions. If a new employee shows little interest in doing the job they were hired to perform, this could be a warning sign that the employee will never be satisfied working on your team. This typically plays out in one of two ways. One common reason is the employee desperately needed a job and did not think through what it would be like to actually hold this particular position. Another common reason is that the employee accepted the job to open doors to other opportunities within the company, not because they actually wanted to do the job they were hired to do. Regardless of the reason behind the lack of engagement, the leader should have a candid conversation early on to determine whether the employee actually wants to do the job they were hired for, or whether the employee made a mistake in accepting the position.

Warning Sign No. 2

A new hire demands unwarranted special treatment. An employee who comes into the job and immediately believes they should be treated better than other employees can be a red flag. The employee may lack either the maturity or interpersonal skills to succeed in their position. A manager must be careful, however, and separate out unwarranted demands from potentially legitimate requests for accommodations.

Consider the following scenario. You are the manager of Truman & Jacobson Haberdashery—a luxury men's clothing store in Kansas City, MO. You make it abundantly clear to every person you interview that you need a salesclerk to work the morning shift and Saturdays. After one week on the job, your new salesclerk demands that he be given afternoons Monday-Friday, and no weekends. When you ask him why he wants a new schedule, the clerk tells you that the early mornings and weekend shifts are interfering with his classes and social life. Now consider the same scenario, except the employee tells you that they have a medical condition that makes it difficult for them to get to work early in the morning.

The first clerk clearly wants to be treated better than others. If you believe this employee has the potential to be a superstar, you may be inclined to grant the employee's request. It would certainly be reasonable, however, to tell this employee that you will not change his schedule for the foreseeable future and he has to either commit to the schedule he agreed to, or you will find another clerk who will. The second clerk's request requires that the manager elevate the issue to HR immediately. As discussed in Chapter 12, accommodating employees with a potential disability requires a thoughtful process. It is important to bring this issue up here to illustrate how the reasons for a certain request can carry significant consequences. Managing Without Fear is the ability to differentiate between an employee who may be entitled to a reasonable accommodation for a legitimate disability or their closely held religious beliefs, and an employee who is making a personal request that the employer is under no legal obligation to grant.

Warning Sign No. 3

The new employee disregards the employer's policies and procedures. A new employee who shows little respect for the employer's established policies and procedures will likely not stick around too long, and could be a harbinger of more serious concerns. This warning sign is particularly noticeable in jobs that are subject to strict compliance rules and regulations (e.g., financial services, pharmaceutical and medical device sales, energy, transportation, etc.). A new employee who shows a willingness to cut corners to make a sale or expedite a project is doing so either out of ignorance (they simply don't know what they don't know), because they picked up bad habits at their prior job, or because they know the regulations yet decide to skirt them anyways. If it is one of the first two reasons, early intervention and training may resolve the issue. If it is the third reason, separating the employee before things get out of hand may be the best course of action.

Warning Sign No. 4

The employee is unable to do the job they were hired to do. Few managers can realistically expect that their new hire is going to be a superstar on Day One. We hire most employees with the understanding that we will need to train them to do the job, and that they may need to sharpen certain skills in order to be successful. But what happens if the new employee shows serious deficiencies in core areas? What if the employee has a great attitude, but is simply unable to perform foundational skills necessary to do the job? If this warning sign presents itself, it is useful to have a candid conversation with the employee where you review the job description and determine whether the skill deficiencies can be resolved through on-the-job training. If not, perhaps the new employee bit off more than they could chew and needs to look for a new job.

Warning Sign No. 5

The employee is a walking time bomb. Dr. Seth Myers, a psychologist who dispenses dating advice, writes about behaviors to watch for when on a date that may portend problems if you stay in the relationship. One thing to look out for is rude or obnoxious behavior when speaking to a waiter. According to Dr. Myers, a person who acts in such a manner during a date, when presumably everyone should be on their best behavior, is motivated by two things. First, they want to be seen as entitled, deserving of special treatment, and demanding. Second, they want to see whether the person they are dating will put up with their behavior. Faced with this situation, Dr. Myers recommends dumping the date ASAP.

While the workplace is not the dating scene—and generally should never be, as we will discuss later in this book—there are some similarities between dating and the fusion stage. Just as it is wise not to strike up a romance with someone who is obnoxious to a waiter, it usually makes sense to separate a new hire who exhibits toxic behaviors toward their coworkers. Just because someone has the tendency to be a bully or jerk does not necessarily mean that they will become an illegal harasser or discriminator. Such behaviors, particularly early on, however, should raise concerns that the new hire is introducing toxic behaviors at work. An early and serious intervention is necessary before the new employee affects morale or worse, engages in illegal behaviors.

OBJECTIVE FIVE: GOAL SETTING

By this point in the fusion stage, the new hire is beginning to assimilate into the organization's work culture. They have a good grasp of the skills they need to work on to succeed in their position, and understand how to safely and properly do their job. Now, several months into the employment relationship (assuming the new hire has made it this far), the leader has the opportunity to establish goals for the employee going forward. Setting goals for an employee is one of the most challenging aspects of people management. Set the bar too low, and the employee is not sufficiently challenged. Set the bar too high, and you are setting the employee up for failure.

Goal setting at the end of the fusion stage should be less concerned with tangible metrics (which should instead be the focus of performance reviews), and more about creating an opportunity for the employee and their manager to be on the same page going forward. By the end of the fusion stage, a new employee should be able to answer four important questions:

1. What does it take to be successful on this team?
2. What does it take to be successful in this organization?
3. What rules and procedures do I need to abide by as an employee of this organization?
4. How will my leader support my professional development going forward?

If you have led the new employee through a successful fusion stage, the new employee should easily be able to respond to all four questions.

• • • • • • • • • • •
MANAGING WITHOUT FEAR PLAYBOOK

How to Make the Most of Your Employees' First Three Months on the Job

1. Spend time conveying the organization's culture by having a series of discussions about the organization's mission, core values, and workplace culture.
2. Teach and coach new employees on how to do the job they were hired to do and how to help you, as their manager, be successful.
3. Spend time educating (and showing) new employees how to comply with your organization's policies and procedures.
4. Provide new employees with regular assessment and feedback during this critical fusion stage.

CHAPTER 7

Lawfully Drafting and Conducting Employee Performance Reviews

Perhaps only second to filing taxes, drafting annual employee evaluations may be the least enjoyable task a manager has to do every year. The chief people officer for a large online retailer facetiously told me that she hears a cacophonous groan every year the second her email reminding managers to complete performance evaluations hits their inboxes. Why is completing annual evaluations often such an anxiety-inducing experience for managers? Why do managers tend to procrastinate, waiting until the last few days to complete evaluations? All of this begs the question: Why do employers require managers to spend so much time and energy completing evaluations in the first place?

Evaluating others is easier said than done. Put a group of managers around a table over dinner and a few drinks and they will have no problem complaining about their subordinates. Likewise, it is easy for managers to bestow praise on their most cherished employees. But to actually think critically about how another employee performed over a period of time, and provide constructive criticism, can be a particularly challenging and daunting undertaking. In this chapter, we will explore why a leader who strives to manage without fear needs to pay careful attention to how they lawfully and effectively evaluate their employees' performance.

A HISTORICAL OVERVIEW

For millennia, employees toiled in the fields, apprenticed with a master craftsman, and bartered goods, all without ever having to sit through an annual performance evaluation. Not that this was somehow the golden age of employer-employee relations. Far from it. With the exception of the relatively few laborers who had enough resources and clout to move from one job to another, most workers (feudal serfs, indentured servants, and of course slaves, to name a few) were required to do what their "masters" told them to do.

The idea that employers should formally evaluate an employee's performance is a relatively recent phenomenon—from the early twentieth century. Labor historians credit Frederick Winslow Taylor with the invention of modern management theory and a formalized system to evaluate employee performance.

In 1911, Taylor penned *The Principles of Scientific Management*, in which he advanced the idea of using "scientific methods" in the workplace, and specifically the post–Industrial Revolution American factory. In what eventually become known as Taylorism, he wrote that the U.S. economy overall and the entire country (he had a flare for the dramatic) was horribly inefficient. Taylor blamed this inefficiency on a failure by managers to apply engineering principles to humans. He observed that most companies at the time made hiring decisions because a particular candidate "looked like the right man." Instead, he posited, employers should focus on how to train employees to fit within a scientific system that puts efficiency and quality above everything else. Taylor's relentless focus on training employees on how to be more productive in a factory environment seeded America's rise as an economic giant in the twentieth century. It also led to modern management theory, and specifically the idea that employers should provide formalized feedback, often based on comparative metrics, as part of an annual performance review.

While fascinating, the historical background of the development of performance evaluations does not answer two important questions relating to why U.S. employers have nearly universally adopted annual performance evaluations:

- If most employees are "at-will"—and therefore can be terminated for *any* reason so long as it is not unlawful—why have formal performance reviews at all?
- Given the amount of time and energy that goes into preparing, writing, and delivering annual performance evaluations, is it even worth the effort?

It is important to seriously address both of these questions. "That is the way we have always done it" is not a sufficient reason to maintain this particular work tradition. There are plenty of practices we have abandoned in the workplace because they have outlived their time (e.g., strict gendered dress codes, dictation, etc.). For the sake of transparency, as you will see below, I am a proponent of leaders completing substantive annual performance evaluations. Not because it is important to perpetuate the status quo, but because well-written performance reviews are an essential tool in the Managing Without Fear toolbox.

WHY SHOULD AT-WILL EMPLOYEES BE GIVEN PERFORMANCE REVIEWS?

I was initially going to name this book *Employment Law Confidential*—a subtle play on the title of one of my favorite behind-the-scenes books, *Kitchen Confidential*, written by the late and great chef, food critic, world traveler, and TV personality Anthony Bourdain. In *Kitchen Confidential*, Bourdain shines a light on the realities of working in a busy restaurant. Peeling back the mystique of fine dining, Bourdain effectively transports readers into the caustic, loud, hypermasculine, and often punishing professional kitchen.

As Bourdain did with restaurants, one of my objectives in this book is to provide readers a behind-the-scenes look into how HR professionals and employment lawyers *actually* evaluate issues in the workplace. Having this unique perspective, managers can forge a stronger relationship with their HR business partners and can improve their understanding as to why their employer makes certain decisions.

Perhaps the most important behind-the-scenes lesson of this book is that just because the law treats most employees as "at-will," many employers in reality consciously or otherwise require a heightened standard to separate an employee—somewhere on the spectrum between no reason at all and "for cause." As discussed in Chapter 2, when a manager seeks permission to part ways with an underperforming employee, one of the first questions HR asks is whether the reasons for the separation are documented in the employee's most recent performance review. If the most recent employment review does not address the employee's deficiencies and/or there is a lack of other documentation, HR often (though not always) requires further justification from the manager. The manager typically needs to spend more time detailing in writing the reasons why the underperforming at-will employee should be disciplined and ultimately separated.

I will be the first to admit that starting a discussion on the value of quality performance reviews by focusing on separating underperforming employees is rather cynical. A leader who manages without fear, however, knows that every single performance review they sign off on has the potential of being put under a microscope by the human resource department and possibly by an attorney during litigation. When an ex-employee claims they were mistreated by their manager years ago, often the only (and typically the best) written evidence to prove that the employee was treated lawfully is the written performance evaluations. Having advised companies in thousands of difficult employee separation decisions, I have concluded that quality performance reviews can save an employer tens of thousands of dollars in litigation costs and can protect a leader's reputation and career. Managers who devote the time preparing comprehensive and accurate performance reviews for their team members are much less likely to be embroiled in expensive and protracted employment litigation. That reason, along with the impact quality reviews have on employee performance as discussed below, should motivate every manager to take written employee performance evaluations *very* seriously.

ARE EMPLOYMENT REVIEWS WORTH IT?

Setting litigation avoidance and a leader's own job security aside, are performance reviews an effective tool to actually motivate employee performance? Are they worth the time and energy it takes to document an employee's performance? Should employers devote considerable resources in employee productivity and HR support on annual performance reviews? The answer to these questions requires a classic lawyer response: it depends. Poorly drafted and rote performance reviews are usually a waste of time and can be counterproductive. On the other hand, quality performance reviews can be transformational.

A recent poll suggests that for the vast majority of employees in the United States, performance reviews do not play a significant role in their professional development. When asked by Gallup, only 14 percent of employees answered that they "strongly agree" that performance reviews inspire them to be better employees.[1] Even more concerning, according to the study, is that about one-third of the time an employee responds to a performance review with worse performance. Just because many employers are not effectively using the performance review as a tool to manage employees, however, does not mean that employers should throw out the proverbial baby with the bathwater. Leadership should instead encourage frontline managers to double down on their efforts by focusing on the following five attributes of a quality annual performance review:

1. Provide Regular Feedback Using the Simple 1+1 Method

Your employees crave feedback, especially feedback that is constructive. The problem is that managers tend to be terrible at giving feedback, especially feedback that can be deemed negative. In a 2014 *Harvard Business Review* article written by leadership consultants Jack Zenger and Joseph Folkman, they found that when employees were asked whether they prefer corrective feedback or praise and recognition, 57 percent of employees surveyed prefer corrective feedback, while only 43 percent prefer praise/recognition.[2] Along those same lines, Zenger and Folkman also found that 72 percent of employees believe they would improve their performance if their managers devoted more time to giving them constructive criticism. These findings should not surprise experienced managers.

Strong managers know that regular feedback is key to fostering a productive, efficient, and motivated workforce. The difficulty lies in how to find the time to give such feedback. Equally as challenging is how to create a space for employees to receive negative feedback. To face this challenge head-on, leaders should consider incorporating a simple technique when giving feedback: the 1+1 method. The idea is that when managers provide feedback to employees, they should make a habit of praising the employee for one thing and then offering one piece of constructive criticism—unless there is absolutely nothing to praise.* Let's say one of the employees on your team just completed an important project for your review, and it was good but not great. Rather than shooting off a quick email with "thanks," "good job," "it's late," or "this is not what I asked for," reflect for a few moments and provide a comment on what was positive and some substantive feedback on how the employee can improve going forward. Here is an example to replace the "thanks" email:

> 1: Nice job analyzing the financials to determine how many widgets we need to produce next quarter.

> + 1: Unfortunately, there were several misspellings and grammar errors in the report. You need to pay more attention on proofreading your work. Let's discuss this afternoon.

It is that simple. Positive feedback and constructive criticism given in two sentences, on a regular basis, always paired together.

The 1+1 method accomplishes four important objectives for any leader who strives to manage without fear. First, it reminds managers that they are in that role to teach and evaluate on a regular basis. The reason why most employees do not find their annual performance reviews to be particularly useful is that, without regular feedback, any constructive criticism provided feels out of context and often is not particularly practical. On the other hand, an employee who hears back from their manager on a regular basis via the simple 1+1 method knows throughout the year what areas they are succeeding in and what they need to improve. Second, the 1+1 method conditions employees to be receptive to negative feedback. While employees crave

---

* I first learned about the 1+1 Method from Professor Jerry Kang, Professor of Law and Asian American Studies at UCLA. Professor Kang is one of the foremost scholars on implicit bias and diversity and inclusion in the legal profession and academia.

constructive criticism to improve their performance, finding opportunities to regularly provide such feedback is challenging. Committing to the 1+1 method provides more opportunities to have meaningful conversations with team members about areas of improvement. This is especially important in a diverse workforce, where some managers tend to be reticent when they have to provide negative feedback to employees from different backgrounds (gender, race, age, etc.) out of fear that negative feedback will somehow be considered discriminatory. Third, this method is an effective way to declutter implicit bias from the workplace. The 1+1 method requires that the manager focus on their employee's actual performance measured against objective standards rather than the manager's perception of the employee's performance. And finally, the 1+1 method is an excellent method of documenting in "real time" how an employee is doing. This provides HR with a trove of credible written evidence detailing the breakdown in the employment relationship.

2. Be Honest and Fair

To have any value, an annual performance review must be honest and fair—honest about the employee's performance throughout the measuring period (see above), and fair to both the employee and the employer.

Leaders who manage *out of* fear tend to avoid conflict as much as possible, which often results in rampant grade inflation during performance review season. These leaders tend to focus on the employee's positive attributes and contributions while downplaying the employee's shortcomings. I am not suggesting that performance reviews should solely focus on the negative. Far from it. Where appropriate, a quality performance review should heap praise on deserving employees. Unless an employee is truly deserving of an A+ and the manager cannot find any areas of improvement, however, a performance review should also provide honest feedback about areas where the employee can improve.

Managers tend not to have difficulty preparing honest evaluations for employees with significant shortcomings. When it comes time to review such employees there have usually been numerous conversations, and (hopefully) emails and memos, discussing the manager's concerns. If a leader has been consistently providing candid feedback throughout the year, annual performance reviews tend to write themselves.

For managers who find it difficult to write performance evaluations with honest feedback and constructive criticism, it is helpful to use the following prompts to think about an employee's performance:

- The three things that frustrate me most about this employee are: _____, _____, and _____.
- If my employee was better at _____, they would be more successful at _____.
- For my employee to be ready for a promotion in the next _____ year(s), they need to master the following skills: _____.
- If my employee does *not* get better at _____ and _____ in the next few months, their job may be in jeopardy.
- To help my employee be better at _____ and _____ in the coming year, I am committed to helping the employee with _____ and _____.

An effective review must be fair to everyone: the employee, other employees, and the employer. Most of this chapter focuses on being fair to the employee receiving the performance evaluation. It is important, however, not to lose sight of how a performance evaluation impacts other employees and the employer at large. Fairness to other employees requires that safeguards be in place across the organization to ensure as much consistency as possible. This is typically accomplished by incorporating objective data in the evaluation (e.g., sales in the preceding quarter, customer review scores, safety record, attendance, etc.). It is also accomplished by having managers apply their own scores/rankings to a shared rubric.

In most organizations, the template for a performance evaluation is designed by HR in consultation with C-suite executives. The relative weight given to objective metrics (e.g., hours worked, sales data, customer scores, etc.), quasi-objective metrics (i.e., the performance ratings given by a manager when asked targeted questions), and narrative feedback (i.e., where a manager responds to written prompts) tends to be determined at the highest level of an organization. When the template arrives on a manager's computer screen, however, it is up to the manager to provide the provide quasi-objective and narrative input for their employees with the aim of being as fair and objective as possible.

It is worth noting that from a legal perspective courts have long recognized that evaluations that tend to rely on the evaluator's subjective assessment of the employee's performance are entirely appropriate, provided they are not discriminatory or retaliatory.[3] In addition to being legally compliant, as detailed in this book, it is important that leaders pay attention to the criteria that are used to evaluate an employee's performance. For example, it is best to compare employees to other employees at the same level where practical. Generally, an entry-level employee should be assessed based on a different set of criteria than that for a more experienced employee at a higher level within the organization. If a leader is asked to evaluate multiple employees at different levels, and it is not entirely clear whether they should be compared to one another or to others at their level across the organization, the manager should reach out to HR for guidance.

Finally, the evaluation must be fair to the organization. Unless the evaluator owns 100 percent of the business, employees do not work for the manager, they work for the organization. Evaluations must be fair to the organization that employs the manager and the employee. Just as it is unfair to an organization to evaluate based on illegal criteria, as discussed below, it is also unfair to give an employee an inflated evaluation. A manager completing a quality evaluation must be cognizant of the many stakeholders that require fair and honest assessments.

3. Ensure Legal Compliance and Avoid Implicit Bias Pitfalls

This is an obvious requirement. A performance review that criticizes an employee based on improper (or worse, illegal) criteria is unacceptable. When a question arises as to whether it is fair/right/legal to raise an issue in a performance review, a leader should immediately consult with HR. Here are just a few improper/illegal issues that have made their way into performance reviews:

- *Unequal Treatment.* Holding employees at the same level to different criteria is problematic and can be seen as discriminatory. This can arise when a manager is personal friends with one employee on their team, but not others. Managers may naturally gravitate toward certain employees, based on personal chemistry. A manager shouldn't have to avoid becoming genuine platonic friends with their subordinates (see discussion in Chapter 11 about boundaries), but when it comes time to evaluate employees, managers must not allow their personal friendships to cloud their professional responsibility to equally evaluate all of their employees. If a manager cannot separate the personal from the professional, they need to reevaluate whether they can continue to manage that employee.

- *Blaming Employees for Things Beyond Their Control.* Say you manage a car dealership in Duluth, Minnesota. Based on sales data from prior years, your three salespeople are each expected to sell 15 cars in the month of January. Let's further assume that for three weeks in January, the city was hit with successive blizzards making driving conditions particularly unsafe and shutting down large swaths of the city. As a result, the dealership only sold a total of 14 cars for the entire month. While it is certainly legitimate for the manager to consider the lack of sales when making staffing decisions (which could include letting two salespeople go) and compensation and bonuses, this does not mean the manager should blame the sales team for that which was outside of their control.

- *Reprimanding an Employee for Being on an Approved Leave of Absence.* The fact that an employee was on an approved protected leave of absence during the measuring period cannot be counted against the employee in their review. For example, federal law governing the Family and Medical Leave Act (FMLA) states that "employers cannot use the taking of FMLA leave as a negative factor in employment actions such as hiring, promotions, or disciplinary actions; nor can FMLA leave be counted under 'no fault' attendance policies." Because the law governing leaves of absence and employees returning from leave is complicated, this is certainly one area that a manager should consult with HR before criticizing, demoting, or not approving a raise/bonus for an employee who was on a protected leave.

- *Mentioning Personal Issues in a Performance Review.* Managers are often privy to very sensitive information about their employees' health and personal struggles. Unless HR intentionally does not share an employee's personal issues with the employee's manager, managers are typically brought into the conversation when an employee is going through a difficult time in their personal life, such as a death in the family, a serious illness, addiction, mental illness, or a divorce—to name a few. Often these personal issues can have a negative impact on the employee's performance. Out of respect for the employee's privacy, a manager should avoid referencing any of these personal problems in a performance review. Even when well-intentioned, there is no reason to refer to specific personal issues. That said, there are occasions where the manager wants to point out that an employee had an "off year" due to personal issues. In appropriate situations, it may be permissible to reference "personal setbacks" or "issues outside of work" to explain such circumstances. This is another area where a manager should receive guidance from HR before noting it in a performance evaluation.
- *Allowing for Bias Creep.* As we discussed at length in Chapter 5, a manager must be careful not to allow bias creep into a performance evaluation. To declutter implicit bias from a performance review, a manager should be mindful of five common biases.

  1. **Recency Bias:** Focusing on events that happened most recently while ignoring or downplaying events that occurred earlier in the measuring period.
  2. **Halo Bias:** Allowing positive traits about an employee (e.g., how likable they are, their sense of humor, how attractive they are) to act as a "halo" over the employee, masking the employee's deficiencies (a similar concern is "Horns Bias," which places too much emphasis on what the leader considers to be the employee's negative traits).

3. **Primacy Bias:** Placing too much weight on the manager's first impressions of the employee or negative interactions from before the review period.

4. **Leniency Bias:** Being too lenient on one employee, and not others, because the manager has a stronger personal connection with the employee who is being treated more leniently.

5. **Gender Bias:** Allowing gender stereotypes about men and women to impact how two employees in the same (or very similar) position are evaluated (for example, focusing a man's evaluation on more analytical/technical matters and a woman's evaluation on more emotional/soft skills considerations).

4. Well-Written: Clear, Concrete, and Not Too Casual

A leader tasked with drafting a performance evaluation should take pride in what they put down on paper. Evaluations should be written in a clear manner so that the reader is not left guessing the manager's meaning. A manager should try and avoid vague and ambiguous phrases, such as referring to an employee as a "a strong individual contributor," "a solid performer," or just a "poor performer." Concrete examples of the employee's performance over the measuring period carry much more weight and provide guidance to the employee on what they need to do to improve their standing. While performance evaluations need not be written in perfect prose using the Queen's English, evaluations that are too casual or worse, use inappropriate language, can create unnecessary problems for the manager and the company. The fact that some workplace cultures encourage (or at least permit) leaders to provide positive and negative feedback using colorful language does not mean that such language should find its way into an employee's formal evaluations. Given that evaluations are often the only evidence that an employer can rely upon to establish that the employee was treated in a lawful manner, it is imperative that the manager drafting the evaluation invests the time and energy to make it clear, concrete, and accurate. Quality evaluations are not just written for the employee being evaluated, but for a much larger audience that includes HR, other leaders, and possibly juries and judges who may carefully parse every word written in the evaluation.

5. Provides Tangible Forward-Focused Recommendations

The final element of a quality and legally compliant performance evaluation requires tangible forward-focused recommendations. Like a birthday, New Year's Eve, or an annual religious holiday, yearly performance reviews are an opportunity to mark time and make a record of the past while charting a course for the future. This is usually the most challenging component of an evaluation. Providing tangible goals and coaching on how to reach those goals ensures that the employee and manager are on the same page going forward. Effectively communicating a manager's goals and expectations in a performance review is a critical component of a successful manager-employee relationship.

From an employment law perspective, when an organization is faced with a wrongful termination lawsuit it is particularly useful to be able to demonstrate that the employee (plaintiff) was given clear direction on what was reasonably expected of them in the measuring period. This is one of many examples where a manager who performs their job of leading a team with intentionality can unintentionally aid themselves and their employer in the event they end up in litigation with the employee. A leader who manages without fear does not make decisions to avoid a lawsuit, nor do they make decisions because it would reflect positively should they end up in litigation. A byproduct of their proactive leadership style, however, is that it puts them and their employer in the best position to defend against unwarranted employment claims.

For as long as employers formally review their employees, there is sure to be a lively debate as to whether performance evaluations are worth all of the time and energy that goes into preparing, drafting, and delivering reviews. While the debate is interesting, it is not particularly useful. The vast majority of managers in the United States do not have the option of ignoring performance evaluations. Having read this chapter, managers will have better tools when approaching performance evaluations. While no one expects managers will celebrate when they receive an email from HR reminding them to complete their evaluations, hopefully the collective groan will not be as loud.

. . . .
MANAGING WITHOUT FEAR PLAYBOOK

How to Lawfully Draft and Conduct
Employee Performance Reviews

1. Regularly offer an observation of praise along with a piece of constructive criticism.
2. Be honest and fair when evaluating an employee's performance.
3. Ensure that performance reviews are legally compliant. Accomplish this by
   a. treating all of your employees equally,
   b. not blaming employees for things entirely out of their control,
   c. not criticizing employees for being on an approved leave of absence,
   d. not mentioning employees' personal issues, and
   e. avoiding bias creep in the review.

4. Write a clear and professional review. Anyone should be able to pick up the performance review and understand exactly what you are conveying to the employee.
5. Provide employees with tangible and forward-focused recommendations on how to improve their performance in the coming evaluation period.

CHAPTER 8

Efficiently and Legally Disciplining Employees

Perhaps second only to letting an employee go, disciplining underperforming employees is one of the most anxiety-inducing experiences for any business leader. The very act of diagnosing, writing-up, and calling out employees for violating company policy or simply not doing their job poses a challenge for most leaders. The root cause of this discomfort is because leaders are expected to follow the law while at same time embodying two seemingly opposite managerial personas: the strict disciplinarian versus the caring teacher, or what I refer to as the Bill Belichick vs. John Wooden conundrum. For those readers who are not particularly interested in sports, allow me to explain.

Bill Belichick and John Wooden are arguably two of the most famous (depending on your feelings about Belichick, maybe "infamous") coaches of the past century. As of the first edition of this book, Bill Belichick is the head football coach of the NFL's New England Patriots. Belichick occupies a unique spot in the pantheon of American sports. He has won six Super Bowl victories as New England's head coach. Perhaps more than any current or former coach or manager in any sport, he has a reputation for being singularly focused on winning with as little emotion as possible.

One of the best examples of Belichick's leadership dogma is what transpired after the 2016 Super Bowl. Even one-day-a-year football fans can recall New England's astonishing and most improbable victory in Super Bowl LI against the Atlanta Falcons. That was the game where the Patriots overcame a 25-point deficit to force the game into overtime. After Belichick walked off the field with another Vince Lombardi Trophy, a reporter asked him how he felt about winning his fourth Super Bowl. Any other coach who has ever led a team to a championship in any sport in any corner of the world would cherish the moment and celebrate the team's historic victory, but Belichick instead bemoaned the fact that he and his organization were already "five weeks behind" in preparing for the 2017 season. So committed to winning, he could not enjoy the glow of a Super Bowl championship because he was laser focused on preparing for the year to come. And as it happened, the next year the Patriots were back in the Super Bowl, this time losing in the final seconds to the Philadelphia Eagles.

Belichick is a very serious and intensely focused leader. He shows little emotion on or off the field, and is usually seen solitarily pacing up and down the sidelines wearing his signature cut-off hoodie sweatshirt with a grimace on his face. Belichick seems to have no patience for anyone who questions his strategy and seems to only care about how a player performs on the field without regard to the player's off-the-field problems and legal troubles (see Aaron Hernandez, Alfonzo Dennard, and Aqib Talib). His team's credo is "Do Your Job." If tomorrow Belichick were managing a McDonald's restaurant, and an employee accidentally spilled a milkshake next to the cashier, I imagine Belichick would complete the disciplinary write-up paperwork before the employee could find the bucket and mop to clean up the mess. And if this was not the employee's first time carelessly handling a customer's order, I suspect manager Bill would have no problem letting the employee go.

Belichick's personality, job, and record of success allow him to assume the role of the dispassionate disciplinarian. When a manager needs to muster the fortitude to discipline an employee, there is a feeling that they have to embrace their inner Belichick. The employee is part of a machine, and if the employee is not working in sync with the rest of the machine, it is the manager's role to either quickly repair the piece or swap it out with another component that will be a better fit. In other words, proudly waive the Belichick flag. Do your job or find a new one.

On the other side of the spectrum is the great John Wooden, who between 1948 and 1975 led my beloved UCLA Bruins to an unprecedented

10 NCAA national championships in 12 years, cementing himself as the most successful coach in men's college hoops and personifying the model of the hybrid coach/teacher. Wooden, who was dubbed the "Wizard of Westwood," is famous for combining philosophical life lessons and memorable maximums with his zeal for success on the court. Wooden embraced a three-pronged coaching philosophy that was simple in design, yet especially difficult to execute:

1. Conditioning
2. Fundamentals
3. Teamwork

Bill Walton, one of the greatest college players of all time and a Wooden disciple, tells the story of how Coach Wooden began the first practice every year. Rather than give a motivational speech, Wooden lectured his players on how they should put on their sneakers. When asked why he started the season with a lesson that focused primarily on how to properly tie one's shoes, Wooden reminded his players that failure to properly put on socks and shoes would inevitably result in blisters, which would negatively impact his players' ability to practice. This, in turn, would result in individual poor performance during a game, which would mean a breakdown in the team's performance. For Wooden, as long as his players and coaches subscribed to his philosophy and his famous Pyramid of Success, they could face any challenge on or off the court—which all starts with the fundamentals of proper footwear.

If Coach Wooden were the manager of the McDonalds restaurant when one of *his* employees spilled a milkshake, I imagine he would patiently sit the employee down and have a conversation about the fundamentals of securing a lid onto a milkshake cup before ever writing the employee up for carelessness. For managers who have to discipline employees, the quiet voice of Coach Wooden whispers in their ear that every disciplinary action is a "teachable moment."

The Belichick/Wooden conundrum can lead to managerial paralysis. On one hand, managers are told to strictly enforce policies and procedures, resist the urge to coddle their employees, and not question their own authority and right to issue disciplinary actions when warranted. On the other hand, many management gurus preach the importance of viewing their subordinates as teammates, caring for their employees on both a professional and personal level, and being sensitive to how employees may respond to discipline that is blunt but fair. Under these circumstances, developing the right balance between the Belichick and the Wooden schools of management is particularly difficult. If you add to this mix the anxiety of being accused of violating the law along with the time and energy it takes to go through the disciplinary process, many managers feel ill-equipped to take on one of the most fundamental managerial tasks. Regardless of where a leader sits on the Belichick/Wooden spectrum, every leader must know how to legally discipline employees. For this reason, we will explore eight specific strategies leaders can adopt to help ease the anxiety and fears associated with lawfully disciplining their employees.

START WITH A RUBRIC: ESTABLISH CLEAR EXPECTATIONS FROM THE BEGINNING

It goes without saying that to hold employees accountable, they must first know what they are accountable for, and who they are accountable to. As discussed in the previous chapter, fairness is central to the compact between employees and employers. When employees do not believe they are being treated fairly—whether warranted or not—they begin looking for another job, become disgruntled, or pursue legal claims. In similar fashion, when a boss feels an employee is not being fair to the employer—again whether warranted or not—the employee's future prospects with the company tend to be short-lived. To set the stage for fairness, leaders must tell their employees what is expected of them in advance. That then becomes the basis for how the employee will be evaluated in the future.

Every K-12 teacher who has earned a teaching credential in the past 20 years is well-versed in the importance of evaluating students using rubrics. A rubric is a tool teachers use to interpret and grade their students' work based on established criteria and standards. Typically in the form of a matrix or grid, a quality rubric describes what is expected of a student for a particular project, detailing the criteria the teacher will use to grade the students' work. Rather than assessing performance based on the teacher's subjective determination (often influenced by implicit bias), a rubric forces the teacher to establish standards before assigning a project, and then holds the teacher and student to those standards. Educators who make use of rubrics provide the assessment tool to their students before starting the project. A rubric tells the student from the outset what the project must include for the student to receive an "A," and shows what a "C" looks like if the student is inclined to do the bare minimum. Master teachers go one step further. Before grading an assignment, they often have their students grade their own work or their peers' work first, using the same rubric.

Like students, employees benefit from knowing what is expected of them before starting a job or taking on a new project. During the first one-on-one with an employee, managers should consider providing employees with a blank annual performance evaluation. After employees complete their new hire training (or for an existing employee, training relating to their new position), they should know exactly what is expected of them going forward to be successful in their position. As a best practice, experienced managers tend to document these initial conversations. It should be noted that as long as an expectation is legal and consistent with the company's policies and culture, a manager is generally not limited to what is written in the formal job description when setting expectations (although a manager should consult with HR before removing or adding essential job duties to an employee's position). While an employer does not need a reason to separate an "at-will" employee, they need a reason to discipline one. Using rubrics and establishing legitimate expectations early on can help avoid costly ambiguities later.

KEEP A DISCIPLINE DIARY

Timing is everything when it comes to disciplining employees. Issuing a write-up too early can cause the employee to become discouraged and the line between coaching and actual discipline to become muddled. Issuing one too late could result in losing control of the situation. As discussed in Chapter 7, regular feedback using the 1+1 method or similar strategies to evaluate employees throughout the year is far more effective than waiting until the annual performance reviews. The same goes with formal discipline.

For a variety of reasons, managers may decide not to write-up an employee for every infraction. However, just because a manager does not issue a written warning every time an employee violates policy or fails to perform to the manager's expectations, it does not mean that the issue should go undocumented. A discipline diary or infraction notebook is an effective tool used by some managers to keep track of their employees' performance issues. The advantage of keeping track of employment issues in a separate document is that when it comes time to prepare a write-up, the manager can easily reference past issues. For example, if an employee has a tendency to be tardy on Monday mornings, a leader may decide not to write up the first or second tardy, and only write the employee up the third time. If the manager has kept track of every time the employee has been tardy, having actual dates to reference in the write-up makes for a more impactful write-up. If challenged by the employee, it provides a more authoritative document. One word of caution on using a discipline diary. It is important that if a manager notes an infraction for one employee under the manager's supervision, the manager should report the same infraction committed by other employees.

FASTIDIOUSLY ABIDE BY YOUR COMPANY'S POLICIES

One of the worst monikers a manager can be tagged with is that of a "rogue manager." Managers who devise their own policies, particularly around discipline, are destined for unemployment. In the context of a wrongful termination lawsuit, employers can certainly argue that a manager's actions were outside of the scope of their authority, and that they were "going rogue." While this defense may mitigate against punitive damages (i.e., damages intended to punish employers), the fact that many employment laws impose a "strict liability" standard on the employer for a manager's illegal conduct means that employers are often liable for the actions of a rogue manager.

Employment lawsuits where employee discipline is a central component of the case typically fall into one of three categories. The first category is claims that the discipline itself was unwarranted. Claims that fall into the first category often involve a situation where the employee believes another employee (or circumstances out of their control) is to blame for a mishap or policy violation. This category also includes claims that the employee is somehow being "targeted" by their manager for illegitimate reasons. The second category involves allegations that the discipline itself was not uniformly applied. This often pairs with a claim of employment discrimination (i.e., that one group of employees are being treated more or less favorably than others due to a protected classification). The third category is that the discipline is a "pretext"/retaliation because the employee exercised a legal right (e.g., took a protected leave of absence, filed a workers' compensation claim, etc.). Aware of how employee discipline can become a central component of an employee's wrongful termination lawsuit, effective leaders are very careful to discipline consistent with their organization's established policies and the legal requirement that employees may not be disciplined for discriminatory or retaliatory reasons.

Take, for example, an employer that has a so-called "progressive discipline policy." Such a policy generally requires a formal escalation process when disciplining employees (i.e., a verbal warning, followed by a written warning, followed by a three-day suspension and performance improvement plan, followed by an involuntary separation, etc.). Even though progressive discipline policies tend to have escalation clauses that allow an employer to bypass steps where justified, employers are often hit with accusations that they did not follow their own policies when meting out discipline. The best way to defend against such claims is by demonstrating that the disciplinary action complies with the company's existing policies. Whether it is the company's discipline policies, attendance, safety, or wage and hour policies, it is always helpful for an employer to be able to reference specific policies and procedures in the employee write-up. Citing existing policies is the best way to demonstrate that the manager is abiding by the organization's own policies.

There is no way to guarantee that you and your company will not be targeted with an employment lawsuit brought by a disgruntled employee. It is inevitable. Creating a culture of compliance around the Managing Without Fear principles, however, will significantly reduce—and should all but eliminate—the risks associated with such claims.

PARTNER WITH THE HUMAN RESOURCE DEPARTMENT

The best way for a manager to avoid the dreaded designation of being a "rogue manager" is by partnering with HR before disciplining an employee. While companies typically do not require HR approval every time a leader issues constructive criticism or coaching, most organizations require that HR be involved in any formal employee discipline. Regardless of whether an organization mandates that a manager partner with HR before issuing a disciplinary action, or if it is up to the individual manager to decide whether to seek HR's advice, managers should be prepared to answer the following questions before approaching HR:

- Why do you believe it is appropriate to discipline the employee?
- What do you hope to accomplish by way of the discipline?
- What behaviors would you like to change, if any, by way of the discipline?
- What are you going to do to help the employee avoid these issues in the future?
- Prior to issuing the discipline, did you give the employee any warnings? If so, what warnings did you give and when?
- Do you believe this discipline warrants immediate separation? Why or why not?
- How would you like to communicate this discipline to the employee?
- Have you disciplined other employees for this same conduct? If not, why not?
- Are there any specific policies or procedures you can reference to support the decision to discipline this employee?

Being prepared to answer these questions can streamline the conversation and tends to give HR confidence that a leader's decision is sound, fair, and legally compliant.

BE CLEAR, LEGIBLE, AND LEGAL

The graveyard of employment lawsuits of yore that have gone very badly for companies is riddled with poorly drafted disciplinary write-ups. Attorneys who make a living suing companies are skilled in the art of turning a manager's well-intentioned (albeit poorly drafted) words into evidence that their client was mistreated. Most of these traps can be avoided. In addition to following the guidance laid out in this chapter—and for that matter this entire book—managers should pay attention to the following specific writing strategies while drafting the disciplinary document.

- It can't be stressed enough: discipline is not coaching. Effective coaching makes use of a tone that says to employees: *"It is important that you improve upon X. I am here to help you get better by teaching you Y."* The tone of a discipline, however, is typically much more blunt: *"You either violated an established policy or procedure, or failed to heed my past coaching; your conduct is entirely unacceptable and will not be tolerated!"* Leaders who try to turn a disciplinary write-up into a coaching document end up with neither. To be clear (as discussed below), there is always an opportunity in a write-up to be forward thinking, unless the write-up triggers the employee's immediate separation. When it comes to reporting on the reason for the discipline, leaders should not feel the need to hold back or soften the blow.

- Use clear language and provide necessary context as if you are explaining the situation to an outsider. Everything a manager does and writes about an employee can end up under a microscope in litigation. Before issuing a write-up, a leader should read it first from the perspective of the employee who will be receiving it, and second from the perspective of how a judge or jury in the future would read the document if that is all they had to rely upon. The prose need not be perfect, but it should be clear and convey exactly what the manager wishes to convey. Say, for example, that an employee blew a huge deadline that caused the company to nearly lose a big account. The disciplinary write-up should not just mention the blown deadline, but provide context for why the deadline was important, why the employee was responsible for the blown deadline, why the employee's actions jeopardized an important business relationship, and the expectation going forward regarding this issue. While certainly not every write-up will require a lengthy fact-laden recitation, an effective write-up should paint a clear picture of the issue(s) that prompted the discipline unless the transgression is clear on its face (e.g., unexcused absence, inappropriate workplace banter, etc.). If a person of average intelligence reads the write-up in three years, would they understand the reasons for the discipline and why it was legitimate to give it to the employee? If the answer is no, it requires more details and background information.

- Proofread. In most organizations, escalating an issue to formal written discipline is a serious matter. If a manager is uncomfortable with this form of writing, there is no shame in asking for assistance from either HR or another manager in the organization to help put the ideas into words.

- It must be legally compliant. This is another obvious point. If a leader has any concerns about the legality of a write-up, the leader should raise these concerns with HR or another executive immediately.

ALLOW EMPLOYEES TO RESPOND AND FOLLOW UP WITH ANY CONCERNS

Whether or not there is a dedicated space on the discipline form, if the employee wants to respond to the write-up, they should be allowed to do so. If the write-up is well-documented and not controversial, the employee's response typically constitutes a simple acknowledgment and vow to do better in the future. While that may be the rule, the exceptions are when the employee either has a legitimate grievance with the write-up (e.g., the write-up fails to recognize there is another side to the story), or is trying to blame others for their own shortcomings. Whether legitimate or not, if the employee lodges a complaint about the fairness of the process, another employee, or the manager who issued the write-up, it is imperative that the company properly investigate the issue.

SHORT OF SEPARATION, HAVE A CLEAR PLAN OF IMPROVEMENT IN PLACE

Unless the write-up results in an automatic separation, it is advisable to include a plan of improvement going forward. The amount of detail in the plan is often dictated by the reason for the write-up. If an employee was tardy three days in a row, the "plan" may simply be the employee committing to arriving at work on time every day, and a warning that one more unexcused tardy in the next two months will result in immediate termination. Contrast that with an employee who is being disciplined for a litany of performance problems. For this employee, the plan going forward should outline the specific performance expectations and, where appropriate, a timeline to achieve these expectations. Whether included in a formal performance improvement plan or within the disciplinary write-up itself, the goal is for the employee and the leader to walk away from the disciplinary meeting with a clear understanding as to what is expected of the employee going forward and the consequences if the employee fails to deliver on these expectations.

BE DIRECT, FIRM, AND FORWARD-LOOKING WHEN PRESENTING THE WRITE-UP

Unless logistically impossible or impractical, managers should meet with their subordinates in person (or via video conference for remote workers) to discuss the write-up and expectations going forward. Some companies require that an HR representative participate in the meeting, while others mandate that the employee's direct manager and another manager in the organization participate. While not legally required, it is certainly a best practice to have another manager in the room as a witness. Managers who have not had considerable experience delivering disciplinary write-ups may want to rehearse the conversation, covering everything from answering questions the employee may have (e.g., Does this mean I am being let go? How will this impact my pay? Why am I being blamed for this? etc.), to where everyone will sit in the room (Pro Tip: The employee should always sit in the chair closest to the door).

When asked to describe how he transforms words on a page into a scene, the legendary film actor Harrison Ford replied, "Sometimes I try to improve the language, the lines, or the delivery, but I don't ad-lib because I think that makes it really hard for everybody else involved." Much like how Harrison Ford approaches a scene, the manager delivering a disciplinary write-up should be prepared to provide the employee with greater context, answer the employee's questions, and improve upon what is written on the page, yet never ad-lib or go beyond the carefully crafted write-up.

...

Effectively disciplining employees requires an equal part of Bill Belichick's no-nonsense tough love approach and John Wooden's patience and temperament. While few managers will ever become entirely comfortable disciplining their employees, following the lessons outlined in this chapter will ease the stress, anxiety, and confusion surrounding this essential component of a leader's role.

• • • • • • • • • • •
MANAGING WITHOUT FEAR PLAYBOOK

Eight Best Practices to Efficiently and Legally Discipline Employees

1. From the outset, establish a clear and measurable rubric regarding the employee's performance expectations.
2. Maintain a "Discipline Diary," documenting verbal coaching sessions and performance lapses.
3. Fastidiously abide by your company's employment policies and procedures.
4. Partner with your human resource contact early and often.
5. The actual disciplinary write-up should be drafted using clear, legible, and legal language. Because disciplining an employee is different from coaching, the tone of a write-up should be firm and direct.
6. Provide an opportunity for the employee to respond in writing, and follow up with any concerns the employee brings to the employer's attention.
7. Unless the disciplinary write-up leads directly to separation, have a clear plan of improvement in place.
8. When presenting the disciplinary write-up to the employee, it is important to be firm, clear, confident, and forward-looking.

CHAPTER 9

Difficult Conversations

When a Coworker Wants to Have an Uncomfortable Discussion

Up to this point, we have focused on how leaders can effectively and legally communicate their ideas and concerns *to* their employees. Now we turn our attention to how leaders can best prepare for and participate in difficult conversations initiated *by* their employees. Knowing how to handle these conversations professionally and with considerable empathy, while at the same time being able to issue spot potential employment concerns, is where leaders can really earn their stripes.

After removing the time we spend sleeping, the average American adult of working age spends about half of their life at work, communing to work, and thinking about work. For many Americans, the line between work life and private life is blurry at best, and for many nonexistent. While some are able to construct a wall between life and work, most of us have thin curtains instead of walls. Depending on how the wind is blowing, this often means that the window separating our personal and professional lives is wide open. In this milieu, managers tend to occupy a unique role in employees' lives. Depending on the manager's management style and company culture, they can assume the role of mentor, older sibling, friend, and confidante. Provided proper boundaries are established—as discussed in this and the next few chapters—and as long as there is no doubt about the manager's role as the authority figure in charge, managers who are able to foster a trusting relationship based on mutual respect tend to be the most successful in their jobs and less susceptible to being dragged into expensive and protracted litigation. And when a leader has forged a personal and, at all times, professional relationship with their employees, it provides a safe space for employees to discuss sensitive work and personal issues directly with their manager. In this chapter, we will explore best practices when an employee approaches a manager to have a difficult conversation.

BOUNDARY SETTING

Leadership training typically focuses on what managers are or should be vis-à-vis their employees. Managers should be positive role models. Managers should be authority figures. Managers should be trustworthy. Managers should be fair. Managers should be skilled in their jobs. Managers should be professionals. All of these attributes are spot-on. They are, however, only focused on one side of the equation.

A manager without fear focuses not only on what they *should* be with respect to their employees, but also what they should *not* be. Managers should not be their employees' figurative sibling, parent, best friend, or lover. Managers should not be their employees' therapist, financial advisor, attorney, or physician. And while leaders certainly can, and often do, develop a meaningful personal friendship with some or all of the employees they manage, with rare exceptions it is not a conventional friendship. Establishing proper boundaries and setting expectations early on in the relationship helps set the stage for a successful outcome when an employee comes to their manager for help.

In Chapter 11, we will discusses in detail why boundaries are particularly important in preventing real or perceived claims of sexual harassment in the workplace. To focus solely on love and lust boundaries and the sexual power dynamic at play when a manager dates or pines for a subordinate, however, leaves managers exposed and frankly confused when other sticky issues present themselves in the workplace. For issues that do not involve sex and/or romance, drawing that careful line between manager/friend and coworker/friend is paramount. Friends typically listen and offer advice to one another in distress, and may on occasion intervene to offer tangible assistance. When employees speak with their managers about personal or professional issues that are causing them distress, however, listening and giving advice is important—but it rarely ends there. In many situations, managers have a legal responsibility to take action based on the employees' concerns. Where a friend can end a difficult conversation with a hug or promise to keep in touch, a manager more often than not has to take affirmative steps in response to the employees' concerns.

ANTENNA UP: COMMON SITUATIONS WHEN EMPLOYEES REACH OUT FOR HELP

Much of the Managing Without Fear philosophy is predicated on the idea that effective managers must develop specialized antennae to uncover issues in the workplace well before they boil over into problems—or worse, litigation. While there are innumerable situations where employees approach their managers to discuss their concerns, there are five common situations that merit special attention and follow-up.

Medical Issues and Pregnancy

Employees dealing with their own personal medical-related issues, or those of a close family member, tend to approach their direct managers before confiding in any other manager or HR. Managers who keep their ears to the ground often have a sense that there may be a medical or some other personal issue that the employee is dealing with well before it is formally brought to their attention. Unless the personal issues impact the employee's work performance, however, managers generally tend to wait for their employees to share the exciting news of a pregnancy, or the somber news of a diagnosis, rather than bringing it up first.

After learning that an employee or an employee's family member is dealing with a serious medical issue, or the employee or the employee's spouse is pregnant, the leader should approach HR in most situations for guidance on the employer's possible legal obligations going forward. Depending on the size of the organization, the state where the employee works, and the organization's own policies, this conversation may trigger additional discussion and an action plan around medical leave (including FMLA leave), disability, workers' compensation, maternity/paternity leave, or an accommodation for the employee's potential disability.

If, for example, an employee tells her boss that she was recently diagnosed with an autoimmune illness, the leader should not just respond with "I hope you feel better" or "Let me know how things are going." The leader should instead express empathy and then discuss with the employee why it is important to bring HR into the conversation. Because workplace accommodations and leaves of absence are one of the most complicated—and thus heavily litigated—areas of employment law, HR professionals should take the lead in this area.

Harassment

In the wake of the historic "Me Too" movement, which brought the scourge of sexual harassment in the workplace to the forefront of the public consciousness, most organizations that had to reckon with a serial sexual harasser in their midst asked the same questions: What signs did we miss? Could we have stopped this from happening sooner? Were there things said over the years about the harasser that should have set off alarm bells? Like petty criminals who morph over time into hardened felons, harassers usually do not walk into work on their first day and begin groping their subordinates or carving racial epithets into coworkers' desks. Harassers instead tend to test how much they can get away with, starting off with a sexist remark, an inappropriate hug, or a racially tinged joke—and, if left unchecked, ramp up their noxious behaviors. One of the key takeaways from the Me Too movement for managers is the adage "if you see (or hear) something, say something."

When an employee tells a manager that another employee is saying or doing things in the workplace that makes her or him feel uncomfortable, the manager (often in consultation with HR) needs to do some follow-up depending on the complaint and context. Obviously, not every complaint means the employee is being harassed or mistreated, and there are usually two or more sides to every workplace conflict, but follow-up is crucial. As we will discuss in Chapter 11, an essential element of an organization's anti-harassment policy is to listen for the cues that, if left unchecked, can create a hostile work environment.

Unfair Treatment

Leaders should always have their antenna up for complaints that may lead to concerns about discrimination in the workplace. Employees are not required to use specific magic words or pull a discrimination fire alarm to bring an issue of potential discrimination to the attention of leadership. When an employee raises concern that they are "being treated differently" or "don't have the same opportunity," or "are being criticized more than others," this should be a signal to the leader that further investigation is warranted. This accomplishes two important objectives. First, if the employee is raising a legitimate concern of discrimination, it gives the leader—again in consultation with HR—the opportunity to investigate the concerns. Second, when an employee expresses a concern that they feel they are being mistreated, the culprit is often not illegal discrimination but rather that the employee either does not understand or appreciate why certain legitimate business decisions were made, or because the employee is intentionally or subconsciously blaming others for their own shortcomings. In the latter situation, explaining to the employees why what they perceive as "unfair" or "unequal" is actually neither can help improve employee morale while setting a clear record should one be needed down the road.

Whistleblower Concerns

Managers are often the sounding board for employees with legitimate compliance concerns, including those that give rise to a whistleblower compliant. Again, an employee does not need to declare that they are "making a whistleblower complaint" to make one. Words a manager should be on the lookout for that may raise a serious compliant include "illegal scheme," "embezzlement," "self-dealing," "government violation," "theft," etc. If an employee raises concerns about compliance issues to a manager in the organization, it is incumbent on that manager to bring these issues to the appropriate person in the organization—compliance, in-house counsel, HR, etc. Even if a frontline manager believes that the employee is not making a bona fide compliance complaint—that is, the complaint is not being made in good faith—an investigation is a necessary response except under extraordinary circumstances.

Personal Problems Outside of the Workplace

There is perhaps no greater truism about the contemporary workplace than "what happens outside of working hours often has a significant influence on what happens during working hours." While managers are neither licensed therapists nor case workers for their employees, they are often called upon to assist their employees with navigating stressful life situations and personal crises. While there are times a manager may only need to be a sounding board, from a legal compliance standpoint a manager should be aware of resources within the organization that employees may utilize in such situations, including Employee Assistance Programs (EAPs). Depending on the personal issue and how it is impacting the employee's performance, managers should consult with their HR leaders to see if there are other resources that the employer must provide (or may choose to provide) to an employee dealing with difficult personal issues—including unpaid leaves of absence, other accommodations, a change to their work schedule, etc.

BEST PRACTICES AROUND DIFFICULT CONVERSATIONS

Nothing can prepare a manager to perfectly handle and respond to every difficult employee conversation. That being said, there are a handful of best practices managers can incorporate into their repertoire, all of which put the manager in the best position to effectively and legally assist their employees and their organizations in these situations.

Listen and Be Present

When employees approach managers to discuss a problem they are having at work or in their personal lives, the manager's first responsibility is to listen and be present. Absent an emergency, when employees tell their managers that they need to discuss a sensitive issue, the conversation should take place when managers can offer their undivided attention. Once the initial conversation begins, a manager's job is to listen to what the employee has to say. This can be easier said than done. Many managers attribute their success in business to the fact that they are problem solvers and "doers." But this is often not what employees need, nor are managers always the right people to solve their problem.

Whether a manager is talking to an employee about a difficult family crisis or a work-related complaint, the employee, the organization, and the manager are all best served when managers attentively listen to their employees' concerns. Those managers skilled in the art of active listening are able to do this very well. Those who are not need to make a concerted effort during these conversations to show they are attentive, engaged, and appreciative that the employee felt comfortable bringing the issue to the employer's attention.

Do Not Promise Confidentiality

Employees approach managers to discuss difficult issues because they intrinsically trust their leaders. An employee may sometimes insist that the conversation remain confidential. Managers should not agree to blanket confidentiality. This is yet another example of boundary setting. When an employee speaks with a manager about a workplace issue (or an issue that impacts the workplace in some way), in the mind of the employee and often in the eye of the law, the manager is the company and company is the manager. Managers need to be prepared to respond to an employee's request to keep this "between us," "on the down-low," or "totally confidential." The response should empathize with, and be sensitive to, the employee's request, while being clear that in the context of the workplace a manager cannot *guarantee* confidentiality. One suggested response could be, "I respect your desire to keep this confidential, but depending on what you tell me, I may need to share this with HR or my direct manager." Another response could be, "I really appreciate you sharing this with me, and I will do everything I can to keep it on a 'need to know basis,' but as a manager there are some things I am not allowed to keep strictly confidential." On a related point, when an employee makes a complaint about someone in leadership or another employee, or brings a compliance issue to the forefront, it is especially important to remind the employee of the organization's nonretaliation policy.

Remember, There are Usually Two Sides to Every Story

When an employee approaches a manager with a complaint about another employee, it is natural for the manager to believe their own employee and promise to take care of the problem. While a manager can usually tell the complaining employee that the matter will be addressed, promising a specific outcome is rarely appropriate without an investigation. I recall coming across a civil lawsuit several years back that proved this point, albeit to an extreme. According to the lawsuit, an employee (we will call her Keri) complained to her direct manager that another employee (we will call him Shaun) was harassing her by repeatedly asking her out. The manager told Keri that he would immediately "take care of it." Rather than consult with HR, the manager approached Shaun in the parking lot and told him that if he ever asked Keri out again, the manager would fire Shaun and call Shaun's wife to let her know that her husband was hitting on other women. Two weeks later, Keri told her manager that Shaun texted lewd pictures to her. Again, without consulting HR, the manager immediately fired Shaun on the spot and, true to his word, called Shaun's wife to let him know what was going on at work. According to the lawsuit, the manager had been manipulated. Keri had been stalking Shaun for years, and when Shaun refused her many advances, he told her that if she did not stop, he would obtain a restraining order against her. In other words, according to the lawsuit, Shaun was the victim.

The manager in this lawsuit would never be faulted for believing Keri when she brought forward a complaint of harassment. The manager's blind spot—which likely led to his own separation—is that he failed to elevate the issue to HR and failed to initiate an investigation. Had the manager in this lawsuit brought Keri's compliant to HR, a full investigation would have likely revealed that Keri's complaints were not credible and that Shaun was the one being harassed. Being a supportive and engaged manager does not include having blinders on, nor does it encourage the manager to rush to judgment.

Consult with Human Resources Immediately

In Chapter 2, we discussed why failing to engage HR early is one of the main "micro factors" that leads to breakdowns in the employment relationship and preventable litigation. One way this breakdown manifests itself is when employees bring concerns to their managers' attention and managers either "file it away" (i.e., take note of the concern but fail to do any follow-up) or attempt to free solo the problem. Whether or not a manager absolutely knows that an employee complaint or concern needs to be brought to the attention of HR or compliance, or has a sense that there *may* be an HR or compliance issue, the best course of action—and one of the most important takeaways from this entire book—is to involve HR immediately.

Document the Conversation and Follow Up with the Employee

This chapter focuses on difficult conversations initiated by employees, not difficult emails, because employees tend to raise initial concerns to their managers during conversations. This makes documenting the conversation especially important. Sometimes that requires a quick email back to the employee summarizing what was discussed and proposing a follow-up. It can also come in the form of an email to HR summarizing the complaint and requesting assistance as in the following example:

> *Confidentially, Monique shared with me the good news that she is preg- nant and needs more information about the various maternity leave options and other benefits she may be entitled to.*

In the event that there is a miscommunication about what the employee complained about, or a question as to whether the manager properly elevat- ed the compliant, having contemporaries' documentation becomes especial- ly important.

In addition to documenting the initial conversation, there typically needs to be a planned follow-up with the employee. Recognizing that each situa- tion and employee concern is unique, it is important for managers to show employees that their concerns are being addressed. Unless HR intentionally removes the manager from the line of communication with the employee— as is often necessary—it is generally a best practice for the manager them- selves, or the assigned HR professional, to keep the employee informed about the status of the employer's investigation and, where appropriate, the outcome.

• • • • • • • • • • •

MANAGING WITHOUT FEAR PLAYBOOK

What to Do When an Employee Approaches a Leader to Have a Difficult Conversation

1. Listen to the employee, be present, and ask a lot of open-ended questions.
2. Do not promise confidentiality, but tell employees that you are sensitive to a request for confidentiality and will make reasonable efforts to keep their concerns on a "need to know" basis.
3. Remember there are usually two sides to every story.
4. In the event the employee's concerns give rise to a personnel issue, consult with HR for further direction.
5. Document the conversation and, where appropriate, follow up with the employee.

CHAPTER 10

A Leader's Role in Combating Employment Discrimination

Fostering Diverse, Inclusive, and Equal Workplaces

Racism, misogyny, white supremacy, antisemitism, ageism, ableism, homophobia, transphobia, xenophobia, and Islamophobia. The workplace, of course, has never been immune to the cancer of discrimination. It has persisted in the toniest board rooms of corporate America to factory floors and everywhere in between. For most of our country's history, the workplace has sadly been one of society's key architects and promotors of discrimination. Despite the ugly history of discrimination in the American workplace, however, the workplace today is somewhat ironically one of the best, if not *the* best, environments for adults to cultivate an appreciation and respect for authentic diversity, multiculturalism, and equality.

The first amendment gives haters the freedom to spew their venom as long as they do not incite violence. Every individual also has the inalienable right to think what they want to think, no matter how ignorant, ill-educated, and discriminatory their beliefs are. And while we must accept the fact that people are free to hate and discriminate in their personal lives, discrimination in the workplace against those in protected classes (more on that below) is strictly prohibited as a matter of law.

Since the 1960s and the dawn of the civil rights and women's liberation movements, those politicians, judges, scholars, activists, and business leaders who care deeply about dismantling discrimination by zeroing in on the workplace have been flummoxed on the best approach to tackle this challenge. Is the answer even stricter antidiscrimination laws? If that is so, how are those laws fairly enforced? And what happens when those laws are used, as is often the case, by unscrupulous or confused disgruntled former employees and their attorneys in the form of frivolous and misguided lawsuits? And are more laws the best path forward, when we already have a mountain of antidiscrimination laws on the books? Perhaps it is social protest, calling out institutionalized and systemic racism and bigotry, and refashioning the social and economic framework that has allowed discrimination to persist for far too long? Is that a viable path forward? In an extremely polarized and hyperpartisan society, is a paradigm shift of this magnitude possible and preferable? Can radical transformations with respect to economic inequality, which is so closely aligned with institutionalized racism, coexist with free market American capitalism? If the best way to curtail employment discrimination is not by fashioning even more laws, filing more lawsuits, or creating a new world order, then what is the best tool to effect change? The answer is profoundly simple: you, the people manager, are best suited to battle discrimination in the workplace.

In Chapter 5, we discussed how implicit bias can creep into everyday decision making, and why it is imperative that managers develop the ability to detect and neutralize implicit bias when making personnel decisions. This process requires managers to have honest and critical internal conversations. Developing the ability to remove all of the impurities that improper implicit bias introduces into decisions is a lifelong project for most mortals. Managers, however, cannot just focus on managing their own implicit bias and hope that will magically transform the entire workplace. In addition to managing their own implicit bias, managers are also legally obligated to create an environment free of unlawful discrimination. In this chapter, we will move from the inward discussion of implicit bias to a broader understanding of a manager's role in combating employment discrimination.

EMPLOYMENT DISCRIMINATION LAW 101

Employment discrimination laws are particularly fascinating because they bring together constitutional principles of equal protection, 60+ years of civil rights statutes, judicial decisions interpreting these statutes, and complex public policy decisions. All of these forces combined have created a body of law that prohibits the unjust or prejudicial treatment of an individual or category of persons based on the individual's or group's status as a member of a "protected class."

There is no law anywhere in the United States that unequivocally states: "employers may never discriminate against an applicant or employee." The law is simply not that straightforward. Instead, the study of antidiscrimination laws is a study of those groups in society that deserve to be treated as a "protected class" to create a more just and equal society. To make it even more complicated, in limited circumstances even people within protected classes can still be lawfully "discriminated" against at the workplace (e.g., a visually impaired applicant for a job as a bus driver, a male applicant for a women's locker room attendant position, an atheist for a Bible studies teacher at a Sunday School, etc.). It is for this reason that leaders should gain a basic understanding of employment discrimination laws, starting with the following five key elements.

Federal Antidiscrimination Laws

As with the vast majority of employments laws, antidiscrimination laws can vary state-by-state, with a "floor" created by federal antidiscrimination statutes. As of the first publication of this book, seven states have enacted laws prohibiting discrimination based on an applicant or employee's hair style and texture if it is historically associated with race (e.g., dreadlocks, cornrows, Bantu knots, Afros, etc.). Only one state (Michigan) and several cities (including San Francisco, CA, and Urbana, IL), on the other hand, have laws prohibiting workplace discrimination based on an individual's weight. In other words, whether an employer can be liable for discrimination sometimes depends on what city or state employees live in. Contrast this to federal laws, which, with few exceptions, cover most public and private sector employers throughout the country. While certainly not a complete list, these are some of the most significant federal employment antidiscrimination laws since the early 1960s:

- *Equal Pay Act of 1963* (the EPA): Prohibits wage discrimination based on sex.
- *Title VII of the Civil Rights Act of 1964* (Title VII): Prohibits employment discrimination based on race, color, religion, sex, national origin, and as of June 2020, also prohibits employment discrimination based on sexual orientation and gender identity.
- *Age Discrimination in Employment Act of 1967* (ADEA): Prohibits age discrimination against employees who are 40 years and older.
- *Rehabilitation Act of 1973*: Extended civil rights to people with disabilities.
- *Title I and Title V of the Americans with Disabilities Act of 1990* (ADA): Makes it unlawful for an employer with 15 or more employees to discriminate against a qualified individual with a disability.
- *Genetic Information Nondiscrimination Act of 2008* (GINA): Prohibits employment discrimination based on genetic information.

The Protected Classes

Most antidiscrimination laws are intended to help right historical wrongs by providing additional legal protections to groups who have historically faced, and often continue to face, discrimination in the workplace due to their immutable characteristics. This includes laws prohibiting discrimination based on one's race, sex, national origin, ethnicity, sexual orientation, sexual identity, age, and genetic differences. Antidiscrimination laws also protect individuals who face unique obstacles at work due to their physical and mental disabilities, as well as those groups lawmakers specifically identified as deserving of antidiscrimination protections, such as veterans, visa holders, and people with closely held religious beliefs. In addition to the federal protected classes of sex, sexual orientation/identity, race, age (over 40), disability, pregnancy, color, creed, national origin, religion, veteran status, familial status, and genetic information, many states have added to, and continue to develop, additional protected classifications. For example, as I write this, California law provides various protections based on religious dress and grooming, marital status, political affiliation, victims of domestic abuse and stalking, and those who take protected FMLA leave in addition to the federal protected classes.

Legal Theories of Unlawful Discrimination

To fully grasp how to foster a workplace that is inhospitable to illegal discrimination, it is important that managers understand the legal basis for employment discrimination claims as manifested in both disparate treatment and disparate impact theories of liability.

Disparate Treatment

Disparate treatment is a straightforward concept: without a legal justification, employers may not treat applicants or employees differently *because* of their membership in a protected class. Disparate treatment is intentional discrimination. The analysis focuses on whether the employer's actions (substitute manager for employer in this context) were motivated by discriminatory intent.

Absent glaring direct evidence of discrimination (e.g., a company policy or practice that on its face is discriminatory or unmistaken direct evidence of discriminatory animus), courts generally analyze disparate treatment claims by way of the "*McDonnell Douglas*" test (named after a famous 1973 U.S. Supreme Court decision).

Under *McDonnell Douglas*, the employee must initially establish a "*prima facie*" case (i.e., a claim sufficient to raise a presumption of wrongdoing, which the employer can disprove or rebut). To show a *prima facie* case of disparate treatment, the current or former employee must prove:

1. They belong to a protected class (and sometimes also establish that the employer or alleged discriminator knew or perceived that the employee belonged to that class)
2. The employee was performing according to the employer's legitimate expectations (or in the case of an applicant that the employee was qualified for the position applied for)

3. The employee suffered an "adverse employment action" (e.g., separated, demoted, experienced a material reduction in hours, was constructively terminated)

4. Similarly situated employees were treated more favorably, or other circumstances surrounding the adverse employment action gave rise to an inference of discrimination[1]

Second, under the *McDonnell Douglas* test, provided the employee can establish their *prima facie* case (Latin for "at first look" or "on its face"), the burden shifts to the employer to provide a "legitimate, nondiscriminatory reason for the adverse employment action."[2] Even if the manager truly did not act with discriminatory intent, employment discrimination cases often hinge on whether the manager and employer can show, based on actual credible evidence, that the hiring decision or adverse employment action was based on a "legitimate nondiscriminatory reason." Although an employer technically does not need a reason to separate an at-will employee, this is why (in practical terms) HR often expects that a manager must articulate the legitimate nondiscriminatory reasons for the decision before approving a demotion or separation.

With that said, it is the employer's/manager's honest belief in the stated reasons for the adverse employment action and "not the objective truth or falsity of the underlying facts that is at issue."[3] As a result, the employer's true reasons need not necessarily have been wise or correct. The ultimate issue is whether the employer acted with a motive to illegally discriminate. To prove that a reason was "legitimate," the employer is not required to show that it was the "best," "most credible," or even the "right" decision, as long as the reasons are "facially unrelated to prohibited bias."[4]

Third, if the employer meets this burden (i.e., articulates a legitimate nondiscriminatory reason), then the burden shifts back to the employee, who must prove that the employer engaged in intentional discrimination. To satisfy this burden, the employee must present evidence showing (1) the employer's stated reason was untrue or pretextual (i.e., not the real reason but a cover-up for discriminatory intent), (2) the employer acted with a discriminatory animus toward the employee, or (3) a combination of the two.

If the employee/plaintiff satisfies this burden, they may be entitled to ask the jury to award a variety of damages, including back pay (lost wages from the date of the adverse employment action to trial), front pay (future earnings), emotional distress, medical bills (often related to the emotional distress), and in some cases punitive damages (that is, damages to punish the employer and ostensibly teach a lesson). Under current federal law, managers may not be held personally liable if they are found to have discriminated against an applicant or employee. A number of states, however, allow plaintiffs to assert claims against supervisors and managers on the theory that they "aided and abetted" in the discrimination (e.g., NY, NJ, MA, OH, OR, WA, etc.).

Disparate Impact

Where disparate treatment focuses on intentional discrimination, disparate impact is often viewed as unintentional discrimination. In a disparate impact case, the applicant or employee typically cites a facially neutral policy, but when the policy is applied to the employee or group of employees in a particular protected class, the applicant or employee argues that it has an adverse impact on them. To prevail on a disparate impact theory, the employee usually need not show that every member of the class was adversely impacted by the policy, but that a statistically significant number were.

Disparate impact cases have challenged a variety of practices, including for example: (a) pre-employment or promotion exams which, due to claimed biases in the test itself, substantially favor or disfavor one group; (b) arbitrary height or weight job requirements (previously used to bar women from certain careers in law enforcement and public safety); (c) across-the-board policies prohibiting certain head coverings or facial hair as part of the company's dress and grooming standards (which may have a disparate impact on certain religious groups); and (d) recruitment practices that favor a particular group (e.g., a practice of only recruiting and hiring from evangelical colleges).

Employers faced with a disparate impact theory of discrimination have four main defenses. First, they can put forward statistical evidence to show that the policy or practice at issue does not have an adverse impact on the class or classes of individuals, or that homogeneity within the workforce is the result of a "pipeline" issue (e.g., far fewer women go into construction than men, or people with disabilities are historically underrepresented in manufacturing). Second, because such lawsuits are often styled as class actions (i.e., a lawsuit brought on behalf of a number of allegedly wronged individuals), employers can show that the nature of the claims are not amenable to a class action lawsuit. Third, the employer can show that each manager's subjective decisions based on unique and individual criteria, and not a company-wide policy, created the disparity. And finally, the employer can offer evidence that even if the policy or practice at issue creates a disparate impact on certain groups, it is "job-related for the position in question and consistent with business necessity." Even if an employer can establish the "business necessity" defense, however, the plaintiff can still prevail by showing that the employer has refused to adopt an alternative employment practice that would satisfy the employer's legitimate interests without having a disparate impact on a protected class.

Disability Discrimination and Accommodations

Discrimination is not a one-sized-fits-all area of employment law. Bright line rules prohibiting discrimination exist when it comes to an employee's race, ethnicity, and with few exceptions—as discussed in the fifth topic below—gender and age. This is not the case with disabled employees. In *some* circumstances, employers may lawfully discriminate against individuals with disabilities (i.e., refuse to hire or continue one's employment in a certain position because the employee has a disability and cannot perform the essential functions of the position even with "reasonable" accommodations). Navigating issues involving disability accommodations is often akin to waltzing in a minefield. Because disability discrimination and accommodation issues are particularly unique in comparison to other areas of employment discrimination (with religious accommodations being a distant second), Chapter 13 focuses exclusively on what managers need to know when accommodating disabled employees.

Bona Fide Occupational Qualification

A bona fide occupational qualification, or more commonly known by its acronym, BFOQ, is a *very* narrow carve-out in discrimination law that allows intentional discriminatory practices if a person's "religion, sex, or national origin is a bona fide occupational qualification reasonably necessary to the normal operation of that particular business or enterprise." A BFOQ may also exist in limited circumstances for employees protected by the Age Discrimination in Employment Act (ADEA). It should be noted that neither race nor ethnicity is ever a permissible BFOQ. Examples where courts have permitted discrimination based on the narrow BFOQ defense include (a) a hospital's decision to equally staff shifts with male and female employees, (b) a female prison's decision to limit certain jobs to female applicants, (c) a religious school that requires certain faculty members to be adherents to that religion.

Courts have historically interpreted the BFOQ defense narrowly, making it especially difficult for companies to justify their discriminatory practices. The most publicized BFOQ cases, although hardly the most important, have been the lawsuits brought over the years by male applicants to the Hooters restaurant chain claiming that they were illegally discriminated against because of their gender. In response to these lawsuits, Hooters has long made a BFOQ argument—patrons go to Hooters to interact with attractive young female waitresses/entertainers, thus making gender and female sex appeal a BFOQ. In a settlement reached in the 1990s, Hooters agreed to open up non-server positions to male applicants, yet continued to hire only female servers.

Managers should not decide whether a BFOQ exists in order to discriminate against certain employees. If a manager believes that a BFOQ may exist, the manager should flag the issue for further discussion with HR.

LEADING BY EXAMPLE: BEING A DIVERSITY AND INCLUSION CHANGE AGENT

Every year in high school, I attended a weekend youth leadership program at a sleepaway camp in the pristine hills of Ojai, California. My memories of those programs have faded with the passage of time. The only concrete takeaway I have from those programs that has stuck with me for decades is the simple lesson: "Leaders pick up trash."

In their words and actions, effective managers model the behaviors and principles they want their teams to practice. A manager picking up trash sends two important messages. First is the message that the manager treats the workplace with the same care and respect that they treat their own home. Just as we would not tolerate trash strewn across our bedrooms, a manager who picks up trash tells employees that it is important to be personally invested in keeping the workplace clean. And second, a manager picking up trash tells the rank-and-file that the responsibility to maintain a clean workplace falls on everyone, no matter their position, title, and stature.

The "managers pick up trash" lesson is a metaphor for how leaders show their subordinates that they are personally invested in the organization's culture, not just the company's bottom line or their own compensation. It is one thing to give a speech imploring employees to embrace a certain principle, and an entirely different thing to incorporate that principle in our everyday activities. Whether it is a CEO of a world-class hotel chain rearranging flowers in a hotel lobby, the president of a hospital comforting a grieving family they have never met, or the entire leadership team of bank marching together with their employees in an annual LGBTQIA+ parade—all of these leaders embrace this philosophy.

Authentically fostering diversity and inclusion in the workplace while avoiding the risks of litigation requires managers who are committed in their words and in their deeds. Recognizing that every manager comes to the job with their own unique life experiences that invariably shape how they address diversity, there are nevertheless a handful of practical strategies every manager can adopt to show their commitment to diversity and inclusion.

CALL OUT PROBLEMATIC CONDUCT

The vast majority of single plaintiff employment discrimination lawsuits allege disparate treatment (i.e., intentional discrimination). An informal survey of race, gender, sexual orientation, and religious discrimination claims and lawsuits brought by former employees over the past decade indicates that the plaintiff's "evidence" of pretext under the *McDonnell Douglas* test is often a comment that was intended by the speaker to be innocuous or silly, or an insensitive joke that landed with a thud. Referring to long-term employees as "old timers" or "the Boomers" can lead to age discrimination claims. So too can an off-color joke where the punchline plays on sexist, homophobic, or racist tropes. When a manager hears such comments or jokes and does not call out the person making them, it could be interpreted by others that the manager is not fully invested in fostering a diverse workplace. The fact that such comments or jokes usually do not support a legal claim for workplace discrimination on their own is not the point. Calling out the speaker in a one-on-one meeting, or in front of others, sends a message to employees that such behavior is unacceptable in the workplace.

BE MINDFUL OF MICROAGGRESSIONS IN THE WORKPLACE

Microaggressions are brief and unfortunately commonplace verbal, behavioral, and environmental indignities that can be intentional or unintentional, and are often delivered as a negative slight, an insult, or a belittling or demeaning comment that can be explicitly or implicitly prejudicial. Microaggressions come in many flavors. They can be outright prejudicial comments, such as when a male employee makes it known to his buddies that he would never work for a female boss. They can perpetuate implicit biases and prejudices (e.g., speaking slower and louder to an older coworker, or telling an African American colleague that they are "very articulate" when the speaker would not give the same complement to a white coworker). Microaggressions can also be born out of the speaker's ignorance of acceptable interpersonal and cultural norms. A classic example of this is when a white employee asks to touch an African American coworker's hair because they are curious about the texture, or when an employee of Indian ancestry is told that they have an "exotic" name. They also arise simply because the person just does not know any better (i.e., mansplaining). When a manager sees other employees making comments that may be construed as a microaggression, it creates a teachable moment for the manager to model proper behavior and educate the speaker as to why a particular comment, even one that is seemingly well-intentioned, can reinforce negative stereotypes and negatively impact the person who is on the receiving end.

DISCUSSING DIVERSITY—A TIGHTROPE BALANCING ACT

Should managers encourage candid discussions about gender, race, culture, and sexuality within their teams? Is it okay for a manager to ask an employee who is an observant Muslim questions about his faith? Is it fair game for a straight white male manager to ask a gay African American female employee to openly discuss intersectionality and her experiences with homophobia and racism? Should a Chinese American manager openly discuss his own experiences facing anti-Asian racism during the COVID-19 pandemic? There is little consensus amongst HR professionals and attorneys on how much or how little managers should discuss personal issues with their employees, especially sensitive issues around race, religion, sexual orientation, and gender.

Even when the company's work culture is amenable to honest dialogue between managers and employees of this nature, leaders must still walk a tightrope when broaching these topics. When walking this tightrope, consider the following steps. First, start by creating a safe space by discussing your own culture and life experiences and, where authentic and appropriate, the challenges you may have faced over the course of your career. Opening up to your employees shows them that you are comfortable sharing your own personal stories, including your own vulnerabilities. Second, when introducing these discussions, let employees know that no one will be required to share personal stories, nor will anyone be treated any differently—better or worse—because they participate in these conversations. The overarching message here is that since we spend so much time with our work families, the manager wants to encourage the sharing of stories and experiences around diversity and inclusion to strengthen the human-to-human connection between coworkers. And third, whether these discussions take place in an informal setting or as part of a structured program, it is important to establish ground rules, including the importance of being respectful; the willingness to challenge oneself and discuss difficult topics around white privilege, racism, and bias; and (most importantly) using the knowledge gained to create bridges of opportunity within the organization.

DIVERSITY TRAINING IS DIFFERENT

A growing number of U.S. companies and organizations require their managers to attend trainings and participate in programs that promote diversity and inclusion. You may be required to read this book as part of your organization's commitment to these efforts. A manager's attitude when participating in these trainings is just as impactful as what they learn from the programs and initiatives. I would venture to say that at some point in your career you have, or will, attend a mandatory training (or many trainings) that you felt was a waste of your time. I have certainly attended my share of pointless trainings. You may have even attended a less than helpful training on diversity. Managers must be mindful of how they discuss these trainings with their subordinates. If after attending a training session on sales techniques a manager tells their colleagues that it was a waste of time, no one would question whether the manager believes that being successful in sales is important. Trainings around diversity and preventing sexual harassment in the workplace are different. If a manager openly criticizes these trainings when speaking with their subordinates, or downplays the importance of diversity and inclusion initiatives, it can send the message, intended or not, that the manager is not invested in the company's diversity initiatives. If a leader find themselves in this situation, and feels that a diversity training or sexual harassment prevention seminar was not particularly useful, they should address their concerns to HR or their own manager.

BECOME AN ALLY

Being an ally of a group that has historically faced discrimination is to declare to the world that you support equal rights for that group and are empathetic to their unique and historic struggles and challenges. In the corporate world, being an ally can take on many forms. It can be manifested by supporting your employees' participation in affinity groups, making diversity and inclusion efforts a part of your hiring objectives, celebrating diversity during meetings, or simply wearing a pin, participating in a march, or amplifying the work of a diversity advocate.

...

In my experience, most people managers support their employer's diversity and inclusion efforts. Yet translating support for a grand and somewhat amorphous idea into tangible proactive measures can feel daunting—particularly for managers who do not consider themselves to be diverse or simply feel they do not have enough time. These challenges are compounded when a manager is worried that one misstep at work may subject them to embarrassment, ridicule, or reprimand. By incorporating the lessons outlined above into a manager's daily practice, managers can overcome any hesitation they may have about their role in creating a more equitable and inclusive workforce. An effective manager is not sitting in the stands as a spectator watching the national dialogue around race, gender, ethnicity, and sexual orientation in the workplace play out. Instead, that manager is doing their part in building a more just and equal society by creating that microcosm on their teams and within their companies.

· · · · · · · · · · ·
MANAGING WITHOUT FEAR PLAYBOOK

How to Be a Diversity and Inclusion Change Agent

1. Call out problematic conduct.
2. Be mindful of microaggressions in the workplace.
3. Discuss diversity in a respectful, professional, and empathetic manner.
4. Treat diversity and inclusion training as immensely important.
5. Become an ally by celebrating the diversity within your organization.

CHAPTER 11

Creating a Harassment-Free Workplace

When living through a seismic historical event, it can be difficult to feel how much the earth is shaking underneath you. This is particularly apropos when one considers the impact of the Me Too movement on corporate America and the larger zeitgeist.

In 2006, Tarana Burke, a community organizer and social justice activist, created a Myspace page for women using the tagline "Me Too." The goal was to help survivors of sexual violence and harassment, particularly women of color, build a supportive community. For the next decade, Burke worked to encourage women to speak openly about their painful experiences as victims of sexual assault. Burke founded her organization with the premise that survivors of sexual violence must have a safe space to share their personal stories in order to expose and curtail violence against women. In addition to the cathartic psychological impact of knowing that other women have faced similar trauma, their collective experiences exposed the horrors of sexual violence. They called attention to the deeply rooted structural forces of misogyny, racism, toxic masculinity, prejudice, and inequality that have allowed violence against women to persist for far too long in this country.

Fast forward to October, 2017. The *New York Times* reported that actress and political activist Ashley Judd had accused Harvey Weinstein, one of the most powerful executives in Hollywood, of sexual harassment. Judd reported that two decades earlier, when she was an aspiring actress, Weinstein asked her to meet him in his hotel room, ostensibly to discuss one of his new movies. When she arrived, Judd alleges that Weinstein greeted her in his bathrobe and made several grossly inappropriate sexual overtures. Judd came forward to expose an "open secret" in Hollywood that Weinstein had a long history of sexually harassing and assaulting women. Ten days after the *Times* article, actress Alyssa Milano tweeted, "*If you've been sexually harassed or assaulted write 'me too' as a reply to this tweet.*" Within hours, women across the globe were sharing their personal stories of sexual harassment on social media using the hashtag #MeToo. The allegations against Weinstein, which ultimately led to his conviction of criminal sexual assault and rape and a 23-year prison sentence, were only the tip of the iceberg. What has become known as the "Weinstein Effect" has forced scores of powerful and accomplished men in entertainment, media, business, and politics out of their jobs and positions of power following allegations of sexual harassment.

There is certainly room for debate as to whether some men have been unfairly labeled "harassers" based on allegations of sexual harassment and conduct that in the past would not have been considered harassment nor would have constituted a terminable offense. The question of whether the pendulum of the Me Too movement has swung too far will be answered in courts of law as well as courts of public opinion in the coming years. Instead of asking whether the Me Too movement has gone too far or what managers can do to avoid being terminated themselves, leaders should instead ask: "What can I do to protect the members of my team from the scourge of harassment while creating a 'speak-up' culture for all employees at work?"

KNOW THE LAW

To answer this question, leaders must have a basic understanding of the legal framework on which sexual harassment law rests. The 10 brief questions and answers below provide this context. Before analyzing the legal issues, however, readers should be mindful of three cautionary notes. First, these brief questions and answers are in my words, and unless attributed, are not direct quotes from relevant statutes or case law. Second, as we will discuss later in this chapter, employers can and do discipline employees, and especially managers, for behavior that may not rise to the level of actionable *illegal* harassment, yet crosses the boundaries of acceptable workplace conduct. Later in the chapter we will discuss the "fences" that many companies have placed around the law to foster a diverse, inclusive, and harassment-free work environment—all which may expand the employer's internal understanding of harassment. And finally a word about language. In Chapter 4, I explained why it is perfectly acceptable to use "they" and "them" as a singular pronoun in the place of "his" "her" "he" "she" or the awkward amalgam "his/her" and "he/she." On occasion in this chapter, I will diverge from this practice, and revert to "he" (when speaking about male employees) and "she" (when speaking about female employees). It is true that sexual harassment in the workplace is not limited to men as harasser and women as the victims of harassment, and that transgender and nonbinary folks are obviously not immune from workplace sexual harassment. While women harassing men and same-sex harassment are just as pernicious as male/female harassment, they are not nearly as statistically prevalent. It is a fact that the vast majority of incidents of workplace sexual harassment occur when a man in a position of power harasses a female subordinate. To acknowledge this reality in this chapter, I have on occasion reverted to using male and female pronouns.

What is Harassment?

Harassment is the abusive, unfair, or improper treatment of an employee by a supervisor, coworker, contractor, or customer based on the employee's protected class or classes. While the primary focus of this chapter is a manager's responsibility to prevent sexual harassment in the workplace, harassment can exist where an employee is mistreated because of their race, sexual orientation, disability, national origin, etc. For the harassment to be deemed illegal, the employee must establish that they experienced a "hostile work environment" (sexual harassment is also actionable if there is a finding of *quid pro quo* harassment).

What is Sexual Harassment?

Sexual harassment exists where an employee faces *unwelcome* sexual advances, propositions for sexual favors, and/or other physical, verbal, or visual conduct that rises to the level of harassment in any of the following situations: (a) where the employee is expected to tolerate such conduct as an explicit or implicit requirement to keep her job; (b) where the employee's decision to submit to the unwelcome behavior, or her decision to reject the unwelcome behavior, impacts her manager's personnel decisions; or (c) where this offensive conduct either unreasonably interferes with the employee's work performance or creates a hostile, intimidating, or offensive work environment.

Legally Speaking, Must the Harassment be "Unwelcome"?

The answer is usually yes. To rise to the level of illegal harassment, the conduct *must* be unwelcome. This means that consensual relationships between coworkers, or between a manager and a subordinate, may not always constitute illegal harassment. However—and it is a big HOWEVER—because sexual harassment often exists in work relationships with power imbalances (i.e., a male manager and a female subordinate), it is important to be cautious. Even if the sexual relationship appears to be consensual on its face, without sufficient safeguards as discussed below, the relationship could quickly go from apparently "welcome" to clearly "unwelcome." In addition, some states recognize the "paramour theory" of sexual harassment, whereby a coworker who is not propositioned by her manager, can nevertheless bring a sexual harassment claim if that manager is having a consensual affair with another employee (or employees). This creates the real or perceived impression that to be promoted within the organization women must be the manager's "sexual plaything" (a term used by the California Supreme Court in *Miller v. Department of Corrections* [2005]).

What Constitutes a Hostile Work Environment?

The law prohibits conduct that is objectively offensive enough that it alters the conditions of the victim's employment. In most of the country, to be legally actionable, the conduct must be "severe or pervasive" enough that a "reasonable person" would find the conduct to be hostile or abusive based on that particular work environment. In other states, such as New York, harassment can exist "regardless of whether it is severe or pervasive under existing laws." In California, an employee need only prove that "a reasonable person subjected to the discriminatory conduct would find that the harassment so altered working conditions as to make it more difficult to do the job." I anticipate over the next few years other states will join New York and California in walking back the "severe or pervasive" test. The U.S. Supreme Court has notably drawn lines between "ordinary socializing in the workplace," which may include "horseplay or intersexual flirtation" (i.e., flirtation), as well as "simple teasing, offhand comments, and isolated incidents" with unwelcome conduct that is subjectively and objectively offensive. When determining whether a workplace is "hostile," courts typically analyze a number of factors, including the following:

1. The nature of the unwelcome sexual acts or words (generally, under existing court decisions, physical touching is more offensive than unwelcome verbal abuse)
2. The frequency of the offensive encounters
3. The total number of days over which all of the offensive conduct occurs
4. The context in which the sexually harassing conduct occurred[1]

Courts have generally held that acts of illegal harassment cannot be occasional, isolated, sporadic, or trivial—although in states that are "lowering the bar" of what constitutes harassment, it is likely that claims will arise even if the purported harassment is occasional, isolated, sporadic, or trivial. Courts have also generally held that there must be evidence of a pattern of harassment of a repeated, routine, or a generalized nature.

What is *Quid Pro Quo* Sexual Harassment?

There are two types of sexual harassment: hostile work environment sexual harassment as discussed above, and *quid pro quo* sexual harassment. *Quid pro quo* is Latin for "something for something." In the context of sexual harassment, *quid pro quo* occurs when submission to, or rejection of, the unwelcome sexual conduct by the victim is used as the basis for employment decisions made by the harasser. The classic example is when a manager communicates (implicitly or explicitly) to a subordinate that if she wants a promotion or a better work assignment, she must sleep with him.

How Can an Employer Defend against a Claim of Hostile Work Environment?

The simple answer is, don't allow it to happen in the first place. The more complicated answer under federal law is that the employer can establish an "affirmative defense" to a hostile work environment claim provided all of the following conditions are established: (a) the conduct did not cause "a tangible employment action" to the person being harassed, (b) the employer exercised reasonable care to prevent and correct the behavior, and (c) there is evidence that the employee unreasonably failed to take advantage of preventative or corrective opportunities or to avoid the harm.

What Does the "Known or Should Have Known" Standard Mean?

Employers can be liable for harassment lawsuits where the perpetrator is a coworker of the victim as opposed to a supervisor. The legal standard is whether the employer "knew or should have known" of the harassment and failed to take prompt and appropriate action. For managers tasked with creating a harassment-free workplace, the "should have known" standard is important because it requires that the manager take "reasonable care" to promptly uncover harassment. As discussed at length in Chapter 9 and over the course of the next few pages, managers have a duty to keep their antennae up for warning signs and red flags that an employee may be a victim of workplace harassment at the hands of another management-level employee or a coworker.

Is Harassment Law Intended to Create a "Civility Code" in the Workplace?

The answer is no. In a famous passage from a 1998 case, *Oncale v. Sundowner Offshore Services, Inc.,* the late Supreme Court Justice Antonin Scalia noted that federal law prohibiting sexual harassment does not create a general "civility code" for the workplace. It is for this reason that to be legally actionable the harassing conduct must be sufficiently persistent and offensive that it would affect any reasonable person's well-being and ability to perform her job. Of course, employers can and fortunately do establish company polices intended to create a culture of respect, tolerance, and inclusivity. That is, while the law sets a high bar for what conduct rises to the level of actionable illegal harassment, employers have the right to set their own, considerably lower, bar. Employers establish the types of conduct and behavior that are not permissible in *their* workplace, irrespective of what conduct may be deemed permissible in a court of law.

Is Sexual Harassment a Form of Discrimination?

Yes, sexual harassment is a form of unlawful sex discrimination.

Can Managers Be Personally Liable If They Engage in Acts That Constitute Unlawful Sexual Harassment?

Whether or not a manager can be personally liable for sexual harassment depends on applicable state law. In California, the answer is unequivocally yes. Even in states where managers are not personally liable for sexually harassing an employee, they can be civilly liable under tort law (e.g., claims for assault, battery, intentional infliction of emotional distress, false imprisonment, etc.) depending on the nature of the allegations.

With this legal framework in mind, it is important to take a step back and discuss several of the structural causes of sexual harassment in the workplace.

WHY HAS SEXUAL HARASSMENT AND GENDER DISCRIMINATION PERSISTED IN THE WORKPLACE?

Like institutional racism, incidents of men discriminating and sexually harassing women at work do not exist in a vacuum. Nor are they the product of a few "bad apples" who think every woman at work wants to sleep with them, or are innately uncomfortable with having to work with female coworkers or report to a female boss. To help curb sexual harassment and gender discrimination at work, it is important that managers grasp why harassment and discrimination has polluted some workplaces for too long. To cure the illness, it is important to first diagnose the problem. Recognizing that the historical, psychological, and legal antecedents that have led *some* men to sexually harass and discriminate against women cannot be covered in one chapter, let alone one book, for our purposes, it is necessary to call attention to five cultural and historical phenomena.

Institutionalized Sexism

Women make up a little more than half of the U.S. population (50.8 percent in 2016). According to the Department of Labor, and based on data collected in 2016, women comprise 43 percent of all full-time employees, and 63.9 percent of the part-time workforce. According to a 2017 article in *The Atlantic* entitled "Poor Girls Are Leaving Their Brothers Behind," by Alana Semuels, 72.5 percent of females who had recently graduated high school were enrolled in college, compared to only 65.8 percent of recent male high school graduates.

Let's now turn to politics. Since 1980, the proportion of eligible female adults who have voted in presidential elections exceeds the proportion of eligible male voters. According to the Pew Research Center, women have voted more than men in the five mid-term elections since 1998.

If a modern-day Alexis de Tocqueville washed up on the shores of New York Harbor and analyzed these statistics, he no doubt would conclude that women earn roughly the same amount as men, hold equal positions of power in corporate America, and dominate our political institutions. Of course, had he arrived at these conclusions, he would be wildly off base.

When economically comparing women who work full time with men who work full time, women earn only 81 percent of what men earn—a wage differential of roughly $800 billion annually! The wage gap between men and women is even worse when accounting for race and ethnicity. Given that women outnumber male college graduates, logic would dictate that the number of leaders in corporate America would be about even between men and women. Of course logic does not dictate much. A 2019 study by the global consulting and talent search firm Korn Ferry found that of the top 1,000 U.S. companies by revenue, women only occupy a quarter of C-suite positions (e.g., CEO, CFO, CIO, CMO, etc.), and constitute only 6 percent of CEO positions. For what it is worth, the only C-suite position where women outnumber men, at 55 percent to 45 percent, are chief human resource officers. The disparity between men and women in leadership positions in the government is even more dramatic. In 2020, women made up only 23.7 percent of Congress (23.2 percent in the House and 26 percent in the Senate). And, of course, as of 2020, no woman has ever sat behind the Resolute Desk.

These numbers unequivocally prove that institutionalized sexism impacts every strata of society, from the lowest-paid factory jobs to the C-suite and the halls of power in Washington, DC, and everywhere in between. While sexual harassment is always a cudgel to discriminate against women, gender discrimination on the other hand is rarely accompanied by claims of sexual harassment (according to the EEOC, sexual harassment claims in 2019 only made up 10.4 percent of all EEOC discrimination charges).

So what then is the connection between institutionalized sexism and workplace sexual harassment? It's twofold. At the micro level, for men in positions of power and prominence, sexually harassing female subordinates buttresses their own personal sexist worldview. By forcing female coworkers to endure severe or pervasive unwelcomed sexual advances, the perpetrator is advancing his beliefs that women are not equal to men. And at the macro level, long-standing subtle acceptance of sexual harassment in the workplace reinforces sexist gender stereotypes. The Me Too movement has changed how we discuss and analyze gender issues in the workplace. Part of this is now calling out the fact that workplace sexual harassment cannot be excused away as "men just being men," and must be seen for what it is—another way some women are discriminated at work.

Misogyny

Misogyny is the dislike of, contempt for, or ingrained prejudice toward women. It combines the Greek words "misos" (hatred) and "gunē" (woman). Misogynists believe that men are inherently superior to women. They believe that women are always subordinate to men. The term originated in the 17th century when an Englishman by the name of Joseph Swetnam penned an essay entitled "The Arraignment of Lewd, Idle, Froward and Unconstant Women." It became part of the cultural lexicon in the 1970s when a number of prominent feminist writers, including Andrea Dworkin, analyzed bias and violence against women. While not all misogynists are violent actors (nor are they all men), they all share a shameful view of the world that men are somehow superior to women. From this perspective, if women obtain positions of power, particularly in jobs that have traditionally been held by men (e.g., police officers, executives, judges, etc.), these women are not deemed deserving of their roles. As a result, it is entirely acceptable to demean, ridicule, and defame them for having the audacity to become successful. As a friend and colleague (who works exclusively on gender equity issues and trains organizations on how to combat harassment in the workplace) reminded me, women can also hold misogynistic views at work, particularly if they have an explicit or kneejerk negative reaction to a female boss or feel "threatened" by a successful and ambitious female coworker.

Misogyny exists in actions, notably sexual violence, as well as in negative descriptions of women. In a 1977 quote from Dworkin that sadly resonates today, she noted that the words used by some men and the media when referring to women are themselves inherently misogynistic: "Women are perceived to be appalling failures when we are sad. Women are pathetic when we are angry. Women are ridiculous when we are militant. Women are unpleasant when we are bitter, no matter what the cause. Women are deranged when women want justice. Women are man-haters when women want accountability and respect from men."

Antiquated Notions of Gender Stereotypes

On a spectrum of bias against women and the causes of sexual harassment and gender discrimination in the workplace, with misogyny being one extreme, people who hold antiquated notions of gender roles are closer to the middle. This group of men are uncomfortable and sometimes threatened by the idea of gender equality at work and in the greater society. Those who ascribe to this worldview may feel inclined to push back on efforts to create greater gender equality. For some men who come from an orientation that women should be subservient to a man at home, applying this lens to the workplace can create an environment where men see an opportunity to "assert" themselves by engaging in unacceptable behaviors. While there is no doubt that many men and women who come from a cultural or religious perspective with defined gender roles are deft at separating their personal beliefs about gender from their legal duties in the modern workforce, it often falls on the employer to educate employees on how to navigate these two worlds.

Sexual Objectification

We live in a highly sexualized society. With a few computer clicks, virtually anyone with an internet connection or a smartphone (sadly including children) can fall into a rabbit hole of sexual fetishes and fantasies. I am not aware of any significant peer-reviewed studies establishing that men who regularly view pornography are more or less likely to sexually harass their female coworkers. *Some* men who are inundated with images that sexually objectify women, however, may want to play out their fantasies at work. Harvey Weinstein repeatedly propositioning Ashley Judd and many other women—asking them to watch him shower and give him a massage in his hotel room—speaks to the dangers of objectifying women as "sexual play-things." As discussed below, sexually objectifying women can also lead to a mindset that men "should dominate" female coworkers.

Power Dynamics

Sexual violence is much more about asserting power than it is about sexual desires. The same goes for workplace sexual harassment. When a male supervisor propositions a woman for *quid pro quo* sexual favors, the overt or implied message is: "I have power over you, and if you want to keep your job, you need to submit to that power."

Now that we have explored the relevant legal framework and several of the contributing factors that have historically led to workplace sexual harassment, let's turn our attention on what leaders can do to create a workplace free of harassment.

CREATING "FENCES" IN THE WORKPLACE TO PREVENT SEXUAL HARASSMENT

There is an important concept in some religious traditions, including the Jewish religion, that adherents must follow additional rules built around the laws to prevent even an accidental violation of a divinely ordained law. This is what is known as creating "fences" around a law. Contrast this with a "chalk on your shoes" mentality—of coming as close as possible to the line without going over it. How Americans pay their taxes is a good example of the fences versus chalk decision. Some people are so concerned with potentially violating the tax code that they always err on the side of caution and make decisions that are most deferential to the IRS. These are the fence builders. Others see filing taxes more like a cornerback in football covering a wide receiver, figuring out how much they can get away with before the referee (i.e., the IRS) blows the whistle. These are the chalk on their shoes advocates.

When it comes to creating an inclusive workplace that strives to root out sexual harassment, managers need to be firmly in the fence-building camp. Managers who adopt a laissez faire attitude ("chalk on the shoes") about preventing sexual harassment (i.e., tolerating conduct that comes close to, but does not cross, the line into actionable harassment) have to ask themselves whether merely following the letter of the law creates a work culture that they are proud of. And if following the letter of the law is not a motivating factor for the sake of self-preservation, the "chalk on the shoes" managers are much more likely to find themselves having to defend their decisions in litigation.

For the remainder of the chapter, we will focus on best practices managers can employ to build fences around existing anti-harassment laws. Those managers who make an effort to assiduously guard these fences are in the best position to promote a workplace free of illegal harassment, obnoxious and bullying behaviors, and gender inequality. By focusing on the continuum of harassing behaviors—which, on one end of the spectrum, starts with bullying and rude behavior, and on the other end can lead to criminal conduct—managers can build teams and a workplace that abhors behaviors that can lead to illegal harassment. These best practices also help protect managers from finding themselves and their subordinates in situations where they come too close to the line where acceptable behavior ends and inappropriate and potentially illegal behavior begins.

TEN BEST PRACTICES LEADERS CAN ADOPT TO "GUARD THE FENCES" THAT HELP PREVENT WORKPLACE HARASSMENT

1. Don't talk about sex at work and avoid any discussions that sexually objectify coworkers.

Preventing sexual harassment often comes down to whether managers and the employees they work for respect professional boundaries. Part and parcel of respecting boundaries is not talking about one's sexual exploits at work, and never tolerating conversations that sexually objectify coworkers.

Consider the following scenario. A male manager walks into the break-room to grab a cup of coffee and overhears one male employee tell another male employee about the amazing sex he had with a random woman he met on Tinder. The fact that the two employees are on their breaks discussing sex is not illegal. It appears that their conversation is consensual, and they are clearly on their own time. So what is the big deal? If the manager does not address the issue, his silent presence in earshot of the two employees sends the implicit message that it is permissible for employees to openly discuss their sex lives at work. Perhaps these employees simply need a reminder that work is not the appropriate venue to share such tales. Telling these employees to "cut it out" or engaging them in a deeper conversation about boundaries at work may be the appropriate response. A response from the manager is certainly warranted.

Now consider a twist on this scenario. The manager walks into the breakroom and overhears two employees talking about a new hire, including a reference to the employee's breasts and how "hot" she is. While the concern in the first scenario had to do primarily with the location of the conversation, the second scenario raises a host of other issues, including that these two coworkers are sexually objectifying a colleague. This conversation is also not on its face illegal, yet it presents another "teachable moment" for the manager to engage these employees in a discussion about not objectifying coworkers. Even in the context of a seemingly private conversation, such banter is inconsistent with a workplace culture that values equality and judges employees based on their merits and contributions to the team, not their sexual quotient.

The same concerns arise when two female coworkers openly engage in sexual banter at work. The response to both scenarios is warranted if a manager overhears conversations of a sexual nature between two employees. It is the subject of the conversation, not the gender of the employees having it, that needs to be called out.

To avoid any confusion on this point, there is no "safe harbor" for workplace sexual harassment. Sexual harassment can arise even when all of the participants in a conversation are of the same gender and actual or perceived sexual orientation. The best way for a manager to avoid ever having to testify under oath as to why they felt it was appropriate to discuss anyone's sex life at work—a position a manager never wants to find themselves in—is by not broaching this subject in the first place. The easiest way to avoid sexual harassment at work is to neither discuss one's own sex life nor tolerate discussions about what other employees do outside of work.

2. Don't give female employees belittling or demeaning nicknames.

Even with the best intentions, calling female coworkers belittling nicknames such as "doll" or "babe" reinforces gendered stereotypes at work. Nicknames can be a sign of endearment between friends, family members, and two people in a consensual romantic relationship. As a general rule, however, they are inappropriate in the workplace. If a manager cannot resist the need to use nicknames when referring to a coworker, it is important that the name itself not be offensive or gendered. If a male manager would not call a male coworker "hon," he should not refer to a female worker as "hon." And while we are on the subject, a pet peeve of mine is when adults refer to their female coworkers as "the girls" and their male coworkers as "the boys."

3. Don't tell or forward sexist or demeaning jokes and never watch porn at work.

Somehow this is easier said than done. Before forwarding a joke, cartoon, or meme to another employee, ask yourself how would you answer the following question if you were sitting at a deposition in a harassment lawsuit: "As a manager, why did you believe it was appropriate to forward this [racist, sexist, xenophobic, etc.] email?" If you cannot answer this question without admitting you were wrong, don't forward the email. I trust that as a sophisticated manager you understand why it is never acceptable to watch pornography at work. The only possible exception to this rule is if you work in certain sectors of the entertainment industry and you have been given the green light by HR to tell and share crass jokes and images with certain coworkers as part of the "creative process."

4. Don't touch.

I have trained thousands of managers over the years on the perils of sexual harassment. At some point in every training, a manager inevitably asks: "Is it alright to hug another employee?" My response to this question is that I generally recommend avoiding touching other employees, and that hugs can be problematic depending on the situation. I recognize that there are times where hugging an employee may be appropriate (e.g., upon hearing of a death in the family). Because establishing physical boundaries in the workplace is important, however, it is best to avoid touching any coworker beyond a professional handshake, high five, or fist bump. And when a platonic hug might be appropriate, it is best to first ask for permission to avoid any misunderstanding. I have taken enough depositions in cases of alleged sexual harassment—where the plaintiff claims that another employee "inappropriately" hugged her (because the hug lasted a few seconds too long, or it ended with a whisper in the employee's ear)—to know that even innocent and well-meaning hugging at work can be later construed as inappropriate harassment.

5. Be responsible and careful when socializing with coworkers, especially when alcohol is present.

Two of the more common "fences" employers have constructed to prevent workplace harassment involve managers fraternizing with their subordinates and limitations on alcohol at work events. This is for good reason. Professional lines can become blurred and boundaries can begin to erode when managers party outside of work with their employees, particularly when alcohol is present. Not every employer has a strict anti-fraternization policy between managers and subordinates. If you are not sure about your company's policy in this area, be sure to contact HR for further guidance. Even if your company does not have an anti-fraternization policy, it is important to be mindful of the fact that even when you are at a bar or party with your employees, you are always wearing your manager hat. Because sexual harassment is not restricted to what is said or done in the workplace, managers must be careful not to cross boundaries outside of work that they would never cross at work. This is especially important when alcohol is involved. If a manager knows that they are prone to say and do things when they are buzzed that are not befitting of a professional, or have the tendency to flirt and lose their inhibitions while under the influence, they need to be especially careful about how much they drink while around their subordinates.

6. Don't date your subordinates; communicate with coworkers who are dating.

The workplace can be a great place for people to find their soulmates. Plenty of successful romantic relationships begin in the office. There is no law that says coworkers are prohibited from dating. I would suggest, however, that for every Michelle and Barack Obama—who met and fell in love at work—there are hundreds of office romances that do not work out, and a handful of those ended up with one or both employees feeling scorned. Coworkers dating on the same team can become a concern, and may require reassigning duties and responsibilities. In such cases, there should be clear lines around what conduct is acceptable at work as well as measures in place to ensure that other employees are treated fairly.

Consensual relationships between a manager and a direct subordinate should be handled with caution. If a manager and a subordinate find themselves "falling for" one another, the manager should bring it to HR's attention rather than keeping it under wraps (secrets are notoriously difficult to keep at work). From there, HR may decide to reassign the manager to a different team, reassign the subordinate, change the reporting structure, or have the manager and subordinate sign a "love contract" confirming that their relationship is consensual and not a product of a *quid pro quo* arrangement.

7. Be careful what you post or "like" on social media, particularly if you are "friends" with, or being followed by, any of your subordinates or coworkers.

What managers can and cannot do with respect to their private social media accounts is one of the thorniest areas of employment law. Nearly 30 states have laws that explicitly protect employees from being disciplined or terminated for lawful off-duty conduct, including engaging in political activities. Issues can arise when an employee, whether it be a manager or subordinate, posts highly personal, controversial, sexual, or offensive topics on their personal social media accounts, and those postings are then viewed by other employees. Consider the example of a manager who posts a meme that is considered offensive toward a particular cultural group, and an employee who is a member of that group sees the offensive message in their social media feed. From that message alone, the employee may believe, rightly or wrongly, that the manager has animus toward members of the group, including the employee. The best way to avoid having a subordinate become offended by their manager's social media postings, and vice-versa, is by having a strict rule that managers should not "friend" their subordinates on social media. The exception, of course, is professional social media platforms, such as LinkedIn—although the same rules of professional posting apply there as well.

8. What happens on a business trip does not stay on a business trip.

Business trips are a petri dish for potential harassment issues. A big part of this has to do with the social aspect of traveling with coworkers, often combined with late-night alcohol consumption. There is also the added element of employees and managers sleeping in the same hotel, which makes it easier to arrange a late-night rendezvous. This brings us to one of my few "absolute rules" when it comes to preventing sexual harassment in the workplace: never invite a coworker of the opposite gender (or of the same gender if you are romantically interested in him or her) to your hotel room. There is no reason for two employees to be in the same small hotel room conducting business. The risks of being in a small space with a bed, often late at night with a few drinks, vastly outweigh any benefits that may come from a platonic visit. Certainly there are exceptions this rule, but they should be few and far between.

9. Take every allegation of harassment seriously.

If an employee comes to a manager with an allegation of harassment, the manager must bring the allegation to HR. If the organization does not have a dedicated HR professional, then the complaint should be brought to senior leaders. Harassment claims are not ordinary workplace fires that a manager should try to put out themselves and move on to the next issue. They are serious and deserve to be treated as such. Avoid telling an employee who comes to you with a complaint that another employee has repeatedly asked her out and is making the employee uncomfortable "not to worry" because you will "talk to him." It should also go without saying that a manager should never say, "that Jim is naturally persistent, but eventually he will get the message." Thank the employee for bringing their concern to your attention, and let her know that you and she have an obligation to work with HR as part of HR's investigation. Along these lines, it is important to avoid telling the employee that their complaint will be confidential. Trying to sweep the problem under the proverbial rug or downplaying its significance can send a message to the complainant that you, and the company overall, do not care about the complaint. Failing to act in a responsible manner can also cost the employer millions of dollars in a trial. Recall that in the course of litigation, one of the defenses a company can rely upon to avoid liability, or at the very least prevent certain damages, is that the employer maintains robust complaint procedures and takes employees' concerns seriously.

10. The 4 Ds: Learn how to become an active bystander.

The last, and arguably most important, best practice for managers to guard the "fences" and protect their employees from harassment while creating a speak-up culture is by becoming an active bystander. As I mentioned in Chapter 1, this book is premised on the idea that providing managers with substantive and practical knowledge of employment law creates a more just, equitable, and fair workplace, which comes with the added benefit of less wasteful litigation. The goal is not simply to avoid lawsuits, but to create a respectful work culture. It is for this reason that all employees, and particularly managers, should become active bystanders when confronted with a situation where the boundaries of professionalism appear to erode. One of the best ways to do this is by way of the 4 Ds: Direct, Distract, Delegate, and Delay.

To explain how the 4 Ds operate, consider the following scenario. You are a sales manager at a prominent software company. You are in Las Vegas for an annual industry trade show with 10 of your employees, as well as your boss, Matt. After checking into the hotel, everyone decides to grab a cocktail before the first meeting that evening. During the happy hour, you notice that Matt (age 50) just downed his third whisky while everyone else is nursing their first drink. While having a pleasant one-on-one conversation with another employee, you overhear Matt tell 25-year-old Joy, a new employee on your team who just graduated from business school, that he had "a one-night stand with an unbelievably gorgeous stripper at last year's conference." You can tell Joy is uncomfortable with where the conversation is heading, particularly when Matt begins to brag about how much money he likes to throw around when he is in Vegas, and that his wife is "totally on board" with their "open marriage." You need to respond, but how? Let's walk through the 4 Ds.

- **Direct.** You step in and deal with this issue directly. You pull Matt aside and respectfully tell him that he needs to slow down his drinking and that he has crossed a line by talking about his sexual exploits and his "open marriage" with Joy. You tell him that for his own benefit, he needs to go back to his room for the night and sleep the alcohol off. You and one of your male coworkers offer to accompany Matt upstairs to make sure he retires for the night. Being direct with Matt in this situation is preferable, but perhaps not practical. Because Matt is your boss, you may not feel comfortable taking such a direct approach with him. If you identify as female, you may be especially concerned with a direct confrontation. If that is the case, consider the next three Ds.
- **Distract.** You can't leave Joy alone with Matt and you are not comfortable telling Matt that he needs to back off. So you jump into the conversation and distract Matt. Perhaps you tell Joy that you need to discuss a new client with her, in an attempt to extricate her from an uncomfortable situation. You could also tell Matt that you need to chat with him about the conference, grab two bottles of water from the bartender, and suggest that the two of you go for a nice walk to see the Bellagio fountains.
- **Delegate.** Realizing that Matt, who is getting more blitzed with every passing minute, may be difficult to deal with on your own, you ask your coworker Sandy to help intervene. The plan is for Sandy to ask Joy if she can accompany her to the restroom and you focus on Matt.
- **Delay.** This "D" is only relevant if you are unable to address this situation immediately. For example, just as you are walking over to intervene, your cell phone rings with an urgent call from your brother. You get sidetracked for a while dealing with a family emergency. Eventually, the happy hour breaks up and everyone heads into a conference room for the evening meeting. During a breakout session that evening, you ask Joy if

you can chat with her for a few minutes. You acknowledge what you saw earlier in the evening, and ask her whether she is comfortable. She tells you that this was the first time she had ever spoken with Matt, and she was not comfortable with their interaction. You tell Joy that you will talk to Matt about slowing down with drinking and that Joy is not interested in having anything other than a professional relationship with him (while Matt's behavior was entirely unacceptable, in the event he misinterpreted his earlier interactions with Joy, it may be a good idea to set him straight). You ask Joy to tell you if Matt says or does anything else inappropriate during the trip, or at any time in the future. You remind Joy that the company has a strong anti-retaliation policy and takes its sexual harassment policy very seriously. When you get back to the office after the Las Vegas trip, you contact your HR representative to report Matt's conduct.

While the above hypothetical situation involves alcohol and work travel, the 4 Ds method would be just as relevant if the manager observed Joy's discomfort in Matt's presence in a conference room, in the back of house of a restaurant, in the breakroom of a store, or in the parking lot of a factory. Faced with this uncomfortable situation, employees too often see it as a binary choice: intervene or look the other way. That is, it's either the "direct" method or nothing. The 4 Ds method is a good reminder that there are a variety of ways to diffuse a situation before it becomes out of hand.

...

As managers who are responsible for creating work environments free from bullying and harassment, it is imperative that we remain vigilant when issues arise that could create a hostile work environment if left unchecked. It is up to every individual manager to decide whether workplace sexual harassment goes the way of the 1960s' three-martini lunch and becomes a reminder of what things *used* to be like, or remains an open wound that never heals. I am optimistic that as long as we remain focused on the task at hand, we are on the right trajectory to build an inclusive workplace that launches us into a truly "post–Me Too" world.

● ● ● ● ● ● ● ● ● ● ●
MANAGING WITHOUT FEAR PLAYBOOK

Ten Best Practices Leaders Can Implement to Create a Workplace Free of Sexual Harassment

1. Don't talk about sex at work, and reprimand any employee who sexually objectifies a coworker.
2. Don't give female employees belittling or demeaning nicknames.
3. Don't tell or endorse sexist or demeaning jokes and never watch porn at work.
4. Aside from a professional handshake, high five, or fist bump, avoid touching coworkers.
5. Be responsible and careful when socializing with coworkers, especially when alcohol is present.
6. Don't date your subordinates and have candid discussions with coworkers who are dating to avoid future potential issues of sexual harassment.
7. Be careful what you post or "like" on social media, particularly if you are "friends" with, or are being followed by, any of your subordinates or coworkers.
8. While on a business trip, be extra careful not to put yourself or your employees in a position that could lead to sexually inappropriate discussions, behaviors, or misunderstandings.
9. Take every allegation of harassment seriously.
10. Adopt the 4 Ds of being an active bystander: Direct, Distract, Delegate, and Delay.

CHAPTER 12

Navigating the Disability Accommodation Process

Disability discrimination law addresses two important, and on occasion conflicting, objectives. On one hand, we have made a commitment as a civil society to break down the many structural barriers that have historically, and still to this very day, made it especially difficult for individuals with disabilities to obtain and maintain gainful employment. Recognizing the historic importance of the Americans with Disabilities Act (ADA), President George H. W. Bush made the following poignant remarks during the signing ceremony on July 26, 1990:

> Three weeks ago we celebrated our nation's Independence Day. Today we're here to rejoice in and celebrate another "independence day," one that is long overdue. With today's signing of the landmark Americans for Disabilities Act, every man, woman, and child with a disability can now pass through once-closed doors into a bright new era of equality, independence, and freedom.

Just as promoting equal access for disabled workers is a societal imperative, so too is the ability for employers to run their organizations in a profitable and efficient manner. In crafting laws governing an employer's responsibility to provide workplace accommodations to disabled employees, Congress, state legislatures, and the courts have all recognized the need to individually balance the interests of disabled workers with those of the employer. Deciding when it is permissible for an employer to tell a disabled applicant or employee that the employer cannot accommodate the individual's disability (or will not for other legitimate reasons), is usually a complicated process requiring assistance from HR, and often experienced legal counsel as well.

With the caveat that, in most situations, a manager should consult with HR anytime there is an issue that involves a disabled applicant or an employee who requires an accommodation, it is nevertheless valuable for non-HR managers to be familiar with how the accommodation process often works, and/or the nomenclature used by doctors, HR professionals, and attorneys when discussing accommodating applicants and employees who have physical and mental disabilities. To illustrate the complexities involved in the accommodation process, and recognizing that every accommodation issue is a unique snowflake, consider the following relatively straightforward fact pattern written as a pastiche to one of my favorite childhood book series, *Choose Your Own Adventure*.

Scene 1: Setting the Table

You are the general manager at a successful 100-employee facility that manufactures high-end camping gear in Houston, Texas. You oversee the entire operation and a team of seven frontline managers. The company is headquartered in San Francisco and has a second, larger factory in Shenzhen, China. The company provides its U.S. employees with generous health and vacation benefits and offers a competitive compensation package. Turnover is relatively low and employee satisfaction is generally high.

The factory employs 10 glovers—skilled artisans who manufacture bespoke and pricey leather rock-climbing gloves. All of the glovers are full-time nonexempt employees who work an average of 55 hours per week. All of them have the same essential job duties, including the following:

1. Must be able to carry up to 50 pounds while walking
2. Must be able to use a variety of precision specialized hand tools to punch holes for rivets, snaps, and buttons

3. Must be able to effectively use sewing machines, needles, and thread
4. Must be able to sit at your workstation for 90 percent of your shift
5. Must be able to read and interpret glove designs
6. Must be able to effectively communicate with factory employees and design professionals to troubleshoot problems during the design and manufacturing process

Javier Castellanos has been with the company for three years. The first year he worked as an apprentice under the lead glover Francine. For the past two years he has held the position of junior glover. As a junior glover, he is responsible for manufacturing the lower-end models and, when called upon, assisting the senior glovers with their projects. Javier has been a decent employee. He currently earns $25 per hour.

This past Wednesday, Javier came into work with his right arm in a splint. An avid rock climber, he took a nasty fall on Sunday at his usual rock-climbing gym, fracturing the radius bone in his arm and damaging the nerves in his right hand. He will undergo hand surgery next week. He is in considerable pain and tells you he is taking prescription pain medication, which is why his sister drove him to work. According to the ER doctor who stabilized Javier's hand, he will have a long road to recovery and will need to figure out how to manage life without the use of his right arm and hand for at least three months, and possibly longer. The nature of the injury and the fact that he is on pain medication clearly interferes with his ability to safely and competently perform his glover position. Javier comes directly to you with questions about his options going forward. How do you respond?

• You tell him that he clearly will never be able to work as a glover again due to his nerve damage, thank him for his service, issue him his final paycheck, and tell him that he should give you a call if by a miracle he is "ever back to 100 percent." **Go to Scene 2.**

• You express your sympathies, ask him whether he has a doctor's note excusing him from work, and let him know that until things are sorted out, he can use his two weeks of paid vacation. He responds that he does not have a note yet, but can get one from his surgeon, and will use at least a week of vacation. **Go to Scene 3.**

Scene 2: See You in Court

You made a big mistake. Terminating Javier after he informed you about his injury was neither sensible nor legal. He will probably file a wrongful termination lawsuit, including claims for disability discrimination, failure to accommodate, and violations of the Family Medical Leave Act (FMLA). You may also want to start looking for a new job.

Scene 3: Get Your Ducks in a Row

You made a good call. Even though you are in a position of leadership as the general manager, issues involving leaves of absence and workplace accommodations are best handled by HR professionals. After Javier's sister drives him home, you go back to your office and call your HR business partner, Alice. You tell Alice everything Javier told you. The first thing Alice asks is whether Javier's hand and arm injuries constitute a disability as defined by the ADA. You learn that under the ADA, an employee is considered disabled if they have a physical or mental impairment that substantially limits a major life activity. The ADA also protects employees who have a history with a disability, or if an employer believes/perceives the employee is disabled, even if that is not the case. Under the ADA, the impairment must be "substantial" as opposed to minor. A substantial impairment is one that significantly limits or restricts a major life activity. This can include activities such as hearing, seeing, speaking, walking, breathing, performing manual tasks, caring for oneself, learning, or working.

You and Alice both agree that the nature of Javier's injury appears to qualify as a disability under the ADA. Alice tells you that this is a "trust and verify" type of situation, and while we have no reason to believe that Javier is being disingenuous, he must provide medical documentation confirming the injury and upcoming surgery.

Next, Alice asks you how long Javier has been employed. You check your people management software and confirm that last month he had his three-year anniversary as a full-time employee with the company. This means he is eligible for 12 weeks of unpaid FMLA leave because:

1. He has a serious health condition and is unable to perform the functions of his job.
2. He has been an employee for at least 12 months.
3. He has worked at least 1,250 hours in the last 12 months.
4. There are more than 50 employees at the factory.
5. He has not used any FMLA leave in the past 12-month period.

Now you have to get back to Javier. Here are your three options:

- You send Javier FMLA paperwork for him and his treating physician to complete. You also tell him that he must take the full unpaid FMLA leave for as long as his doctor has placed him out of work—up to 12 weeks. **Go to Scene 4.**
- You provide Javier with FMLA paperwork, but do not force him to take FMLA leave for the entire 12 weeks. **Go to Scene 5.**

Scene 4: FMLA Leave or Bust

Without getting too much into the weeds, the general rule throughout the country for many years was that an employer must designate FMLA qualifying leave as FMLA leave. In 2014, the Ninth Circuit Court of Appeals (the largest of the 12 circuit courts) decided that employees can decline to take FMLA leave even when their need for leave is for FMLA-qualified reasons. Then in 2019, the Department of Labor issued an opinion letter rejecting the Ninth Circuit's finding that as soon as an employee communicates the need to take leave for an FMLA-qualifying reason, neither the employee nor the employer can decline leave. Fortunately, Alice consulted with the company's attorney before telling Javier that he must take FMLA leave for as long as his doctor excuses him from work. While it worked out in this case, this is a good reminder of why it is important to consult with legal counsel before making decisions around leaves of absence.

Javier provides a note from his doctor stating that he will only be out of work for medical reasons for one month, and that he can return, subject to certain limitations (yet to be named) that will likely last for another six months. How do you respond?

- You tell Javier that he needs to be off work for the full 12 weeks under the FMLA and then you will discuss possibly allowing him to return to work. **Go to Scene 6.**

- You tell Javier that the company is pleased to provide him one month of FMLA leave (letting him know that he will still have the ability to use more FMLA leave should he need it), but that before he can return to work, you will need him to provide a note from his treating physician describing his workplace limitations and medically necessary accommodations. In this email, you also attach a copy of the glover job description for Javier to share with his treating physician. **Go to Scene 7.**

Scene 5: FMLA as an Option

This is a reasonable first step. Unless there are extenuating circumstances, the employer must notify the employee about their eligibility for a statutory leave of absence within five business days of that employee requesting a family or medical leave. The company should, in this scenario, let Javier know he is entitled to FMLA leave. The company may also tell Javier that he will be required to provide medical certification of the FMLA-qualifying reasons for the leave, as well as any employer policies regarding substituting paid leave (e.g., vacation) for a portion of the leave (this is generally known as the "rights and responsibilities letter"). The notice may also specify that Javier will need to obtain a "fitness-for-duty" certification to return to work after his FMLA leave ends, or provide a note from his doctor identifying the workplace limitations and medically necessary accommodations he will need based on his job duties and responsibilities.

Javier appreciates the assistance and is happy with how things are progressing. **Go directly to Scene 7.**

Scene 6: It Is Supposed to Be Interactive

You were wrong. Javier's doctor is telling the company that her patient only needs to be out of work for one month and then he can return with some unnamed limitations. The interactive process must be interactive. That is, the employer must collaborate with the employee and determine whether reasonable accommodations are available based on a number of factors, including the employee's limitations, the essential duties of the job, the existence of reasonable alternatives, and the potential hardships of certain requested accommodations. While a leave of absence, whether or not it is FMLA-qualified, is a common workplace accommodation, it is not the only accommodation. What do you do next?

- You choose to reverse course. **Go to Scene 7.**
- You stick to your original position. **Go to Scene 11.**

Scene 7: Time to Dance

It turns out that Javier's arm is healing better than expected, as he was fortunate to have the best hand surgeon in the state of Texas. Three weeks into his FMLA leave, Javier sends you a note from his hand surgeon stating, "Patient can return to his job as a junior glover subject to the following limitations and with the following accommodations: (1) may only carry up to 10 pounds; (2) no use of his right hand for six months; (3) patient should have the ability to set his own schedule; and (4) must have the ability to take additional rest breaks of up to 20 minutes as needed, indefinitely."

After reading the doctor's note, you are incredulous. It is as if the doctor wrote the note without any regard for the fact that you run a business and that her patient, Javier, is an artisan who needs to be able to use his right hand (which happens to be his dominant hand) to do his entire job. Your options going forward are:

- You tell Javier that his first doctor's note is entirely unacceptable and that because he cannot do the glover job, he will be formally separated after his FMLA leave expires (recall Javier's doctor only put him out for one month). **Go to Scene 11.**
- You tell Javier that the company is committed to engaging in the interactive process in good faith, but that to determine whether there are reasonable accommodations available to him, you need the doctor to clarify a few things. **Go to Scene 8.**

Scene 8: What's Up, Doc?

There tends to be a lot of confusion around doctors' notes and the interactive process. Does the company have to restore the employee to their original job because the doctor said so? [*Generally No*]. Can the employee undermine their own doctor's note by telling their employer that they can do activities their doctor already prohibited? [*Generally No.*] Can an employer ignore a doctor's note that is either so vague or so ridiculous that it does not help the employer determine the next steps? [*Depends on the circumstances.*] What about a doctor's note that appears to have been signed by the doctor but ghostwritten by the employee—as is often the case? [*See below.*]

To answer these questions, consider three general guiding principles when it comes to most accommodation-related doctors' notes. First, without evidence of foul play (e.g., the employee forged the note), the employer should not question the doctor's *medical* determination as to the employee's diagnosis and the physical and/or mental limitations. If the employee's treating physician says that the employee cannot lift more than five pounds or stand for more than 10 minutes in an hour, employers generally should not question these limitations even if they are downright laughable (e.g., a preschool teacher who hands over a doctor's note that she cannot be around children), or appear to have been written by the employee but signed off by the doctor. Second, the doctor does not get to dictate what accommodations, if any, the employer will make available to the employee. While the employee's doctor plays an important role, they are merely there to provide information about their patient's medical condition and the medically necessary workplace limitations and accommodations their patient needs. Doctors can and do provide *recommended* accommodations—in our example they are the ability for Javier to set his own hours and take breaks as needed—but the employer does not need to adopt those accommodations and return the employee to work. And third, in the event the note is defective—as is often the case—it is usually perfectly acceptable for the employer to ask for a clarifying follow-up note. In my experience, doctors tend not to spend much time thinking about their patient's actual job duties and, as is the case here, are prone to prescribing vague and unrealistic limitations.

In our scenario, the surgeon's first note is unacceptable. Let's dissect it. The first limitation states that Javier can only carry up to 10 pounds. The note does not state how long Javier will need this restriction. It would be reasonable to go back to his doctor and ask for more clarification. The second limitation states that Javier will not be able to use his right hand for at least six months. As discussed later, this is a significant limitation, and will preclude him from working as a glover for at least the next six months. There is no need, however, to follow up with the doctor on this limitation. The third and fourth accommodations are especially vague and manifestly unreasonable. The third states that Javier should have the ability to set his own schedule. The company can reasonably ask the doctor to provide greater clarification for scheduling purposes. Because Javier has protected FMLA leave available to him, he also may have the right to intermittent FMLA leave, assuming he returns to work and does not take an extended leave. It is reasonable, however, for the company to require some advanced notice before Javier exercises this intermittent leave. And finally, the doctor's fourth proposed accommodation—additional rest breaks of up to 20 minutes, indefinitely— is problematic for several reasons. Per this note, Javier can decide to take a 20-minute rest break every hour, or even two every hour. This would interfere with whatever job he ultimately performs should he come back to work, which would make it very difficult for him to do his job and for his manager to supervise him. Because rest breaks of 20 minutes or less must be paid under federal law, the company also would have to pay Javier while he is taking these breaks. Finally, the company should seek clarification for how long Javier will need this accommodation, confirming that in fact he will need to be able to take breaks at his discretion "indefinitely."

- You explain to Javier that the company needs his doctor to clarify a few points before considering possible workplace accommodations as part of the interactive process. You tell Javier that it would be helpful if his doctor revised her note based on the glover job description. Javier agrees to go back to his doctor and provide further clarification. **Go to Scene 9.**
- You tell Javier that the company needs an updated note from his doctor before discussing potential workplace accommodations. Javier makes it

clear that he will not ask his doctor for a second note, and also tells you that the only job he will accept is the junior glover position with all of his doctor's required limitations and medically necessary accommodations. **Go to Scene 10.**

Scene 9: The Art of the Interactive Process

Javier comes back with the following revised note:

1. May only carry up to 10 pounds for three months
2. No use of his right hand for six months
3. Should only be on the schedule for no more than five hours so he can participate in physical therapy two days a week as determined in advance
4. Two 20-minute rest breaks per shift, morning and afternoon, for the next six months

With this new note, you and Alice in HR have a long discussion about the glover position and whether it is possible for Javier to remain in his current role despite these rather significant limitations.

Back in Chapter 3, we spent a fair amount of time discussing the importance of having a quality job description that clearly articulates the essential job duties for every position. One of the reasons why this is especially important is because the employee's job description, and the identification of essential job duties, is a key factor in the accommodation discussion. In our scenario, the doctor's first two limitations are concerning. The job requires that glovers regularly carry up to 50 pounds of tools and supplies. Limiting a glover to 10 pounds is unworkable if, for example, one of the standard tools used by a glover weighs 30 pounds. Putting aside the second limitation, however, if Javier's manager could rearrange the work flow such that other employees can assist Javier when he needs to move heavy items or provide Javier with a cart to transport these items himself, then perhaps this would be a workable temporary accommodation. While it is well-settled that an employer does not need to eliminate essential functions of a position, where it's feasible employers should determine if any of the duties identified as "essential" on the employee's job description are in fact marginal, or whether certain equipment exists that would help the employee perform the task yet abide by their doctor's restrictions.

The second limitation imposed on Javier by his doctor, that he cannot use his right hand for six months, is more problematic. Glovers are artisans. They are required to use highly specialized hand tools and must be experts in a variety of sewing techniques—all of which require use of both hands with considerable dexterity. In consultation with Alice, you determine that at least until Javier's doctor gives him the green light to use his right hand to perform complicated fine motor tasks, it would be manifestly unreasonable and impractical to return Javier to his former position with this limitation. Alice advises you that even though Javier will not be able to use his right hand at work for at least six months, the company is still required to look into the availability of other positions for Javier to satisfy its duty to provide disabled employees with a reasonable accommodation.

An employer generally has two options when there are no reasonable accommodations available that would allow the employee to stay in their current position without placing them on a leave of absence. One option is to look at the request, and if there are no other alternative jobs or accommodations available, determine whether granting the request would pose an "undue hardship" on the employer or create a "direct threat" to the employee's (or other's) health or well-being. Undue hardship is generally a financial question: is the proposed accommodation too costly for the employer? Before deciding whether an accommodation is an "undue hardship," Alice should consult with an experienced employment attorney. The employer can instead determine whether there are other reasonable accommodations available that allow the employee to remain employed with the company yet do not force the employer to remove an essential duty of the position or hire another employee to assist the disabled employee.

Which potential accommodations are deemed "reasonable" under the ADA is often in the eyes of the beholder (i.e., the judge or jury; according to the U.S. Equal Employment Opportunity Commission, a modification or adjustment is "reasonable" if it seems reasonable on its face—i.e., it is "feasible" or "plausible" for the employee to perform the essential functions of the position). If the employee's requested accommodation would not allow the disabled employee to perform the essential job duties, then it is not reasonable. Arguably it would be much easier if the government issued clear guidelines for employers and employees on what accommodations an employer must provide based on the employee's specific medical diagnosis—for example, the only accommodations required for a diabetic employee are 20-minute breaks every two hours and a dedicated private space that is not a bathroom for the employee to check their insulin levels). If such clear guidelines existed, the process would not need to be particularly "interactive." It would also not be particularly effective. The law has avoided establishing absolute directives on what accommodations must be offered to an employee who presents with a particular disability, because each situation demands individualized considerations.

If you and Alice determine in our hypothetical scenario that there are no reasonable workplace accommodations that would allow Javier to do his glover job with only his left hand, the next step is to ask Javier if he has any ideas as to how he can do his job with these limitations. Assuming he also comes up empty, the next line of inquiry is whether there are other reasonable alternative options available.

For a current employee, there are a variety of potential accommodations an employer should consider, including where appropriate:

1. Restructuring marginal elements of the job but not essential job duties
2. Unpaid leaves of absence beyond what is required under the FMLA or a comparable state leave law
3. Part-time or modified work schedules
4. Acquiring or modifying equipment
5. Reassigning the employee to a different, vacant position

After considering these and other alternatives, you and Alice offer Javier three accommodations to consider, all of which fit within his doctor's limitations and his experiences, education, and skillset:

1. A six-month unpaid leave of absence (finishing his FMLA and then continuing as an ADA accommodation)
2. A clerical job in the mailroom at $18 per hour for six months (he would be paid the same amount as the two other employees in the mailroom)
3. An entry-level position in customer service at $18 per hour, where he could work from home

Javier considers these options and ultimately accepts the mailroom job. Congratulations, you and Javier successfully participated in the interactive process. Well done!

Scene 10: The Art of the Interactive Process—Part Deux

The interactive process requires a commitment from the employee and the employer to work together to determine whether or not there are reasonable accommodations available. If the employee refuses to participate in good faith, the employer has a strong defense in the event the employee files a lawsuit. In this next scenario, Javier decides he only wants the glover job and will not request a clarifying doctor's note. The process is breaking down due to his intransigence. With Alice's permission, you reach out to Javier and let him know that without more details from his doctor, the most the company can offer him at the present time is a six-month unpaid leave of absence. You encourage Javier to provide an updated doctor's note after his surgery, in the event his doctor modifies his workplace limitations. Javier reluctantly agrees to take the six-month leave of absence. A few weeks after his surgery, he provides an updated doctor's note. **Go to Scene 9** to see what happens.

Scene 11: Take a Deep Breath and Try Again

For managers who are evaluated on productivity and crave order, the interactive process can be especially frustrating. This is entirely normal. Take a breath and recognize that it is not uncommon for the process to take weeks and sometimes months to be resolved. **Go back to Scene 1** and try again.

...

The above "adventure," which happens to be a relatively simple stroll through the accommodation process, illustrates why people leaders need to consult with HR as soon as they learn an employee or applicant has a disability that may require a protected leave of absence or workplace accommodation. It also illustrates something every employee and manager in the United States should be proud of. Throughout the world millions of disabled individuals do not have access to employment opportunities—depriving these individuals of a basic human dignity. While there is absolutely room for improvement in how the process works for U.S. employers, particularly how courts analyze an employer's decisions around accommodations, the fact that our legal system requires both the employer and employee to work together in a constructive way is a model for other countries on how to do a better job integrating disabled employees into the workforce.

• • • • • • • • • • •
MANAGING WITHOUT FEAR PLAYBOOK

Key Reminders When Navigating the Interactive Process with a Disabled Employee

1. Listen to disabled applicants and employees to understand their unique individual situations, needs, and requests.
2. Determine which accommodations are deemed "reasonable" as a matter of law by understanding the legal mandate to accommodate disabled employees, the employee's limitations, and requested accommodations as articulated by their medical provider, the essential duties of the employee's position, and the employer's overall business needs.
3. Remember that statutory leaves of absence, such as the FMLA, are usually distinct from the requirements to engage in the interactive process with a disabled employee.
4. Having job descriptions that clearly articulate the essential job duties for each position is imperative when engaging in interactive discussions with a disabled applicant or employee (see Chapter 3 for more details).

5. Recognize that the interactive process is often a long, frustrating, and complicated series of communications between the employee, the employee's medical provider, and the employer.

6. Leaders should involve their human resource partner early, and where appropriate, organizations should seek outside counsel from an experienced employment attorney.

CHAPTER 13

Wage and Hour Compliance for Managers

If wage and hour law were a sport, it would be baseball. It's simple to understand the basics of how the game is played, yet when you look deeper, it is full of arcane and unnecessarily complicated rules based largely on customs and practices of life before the internet, globalization, and color TV. Like aficionados of baseball who are enthralled by a pitcher's duel going into the 13th inning tied 1–1, and can rattle off all 23 ways a hitter can get on first base, a bona fide wage and hour expert enjoys a stimulating discussion on the history of the outside sales overtime exemption and can recite from memory the types of bonuses that need not be included in the regular rate of pay calculation for determining overtime compensation.

Before I decided to write this book, I interviewed managers, HR professionals, in-house company attorneys, and several of my colleagues about what they see as the areas of employment law that managers need to better understand to avoid employment lawsuits. Not surprising to me at least, the only thing that all of the folks I interviewed agreed upon is that managers need to have a better understanding of their role in complying with wage and hour laws.

Between 2016 and 2019, U.S. companies spent over one billion dollars settling wage and hour class action lawsuits. This number is startling and deceptive. It's startling because of the sheer amount of money companies have paid out to avoid the risks of going to trial in a class action lawsuit (class actions are special lawsuits where a few plaintiffs purport to represent hundreds and often thousands of current and former employees). And it's deceptive because it would seem to suggest that employers cannot seem to figure out how to comply with applicable wage and hour laws. More often than not, employers settle these cases often for millions of dollars, not because they did anything wrong, but because the cost of litigating and the financial toll if they were to lose at trial would be devastating. The takeaway for managers is that most employers, particularly those with operations in states that are hotbeds of wage and hour litigation such as California and New York, are tired of getting hit with these lawsuits and need their frontline managers to be more vigilant in enforcing company policy.

WHAT ARE WAGE AND HOUR LAWS?

Wage and hour laws address virtually every aspect of the employment relationship that requires an answer to the following nine questions:

- **Who is an employee?** Employees are entitled to a host of employment law protections, including wage and hour rights. Independent contractors are generally not covered by such laws. With the rise of the "gig economy," how courts and legislatures come down on the answer to this one question impacts millions of people, billions of dollars, entire industries, and concepts of how and when people work.
- **What constitutes work?** Which activities are deemed "compensable" and which ones are not tends to be a much more complicated issue than one would think. Driving to and from work is not compensable, but how about if you stop on the way to pick up a tool? Must employees be paid for the time they are waiting in a security line to get into a factory? What about the time it takes to walk to the time clock? Or the time spent "on call"? How about time that is so *de minimis* that it does not count as work?
- **When is work, work?** The answer to this is along the lines of the metaphysical question: when a tree falls in a forest and no one is around, does it make a sound? When is an employer required to compensate a non-exempt employee (i.e., an employee who is entitled to minimum wage

and overtime because they are "not exempt" from these requirements) for work if the employer is not aware that the work was performed?

- **How to determine, calculate, and report an employee's pay?** Wage and hour laws are about time and money. To address the latter, how much money should an employee be paid for working or not working (in the case of sick leave and vacation pay) often requires reviewing a host of local, state, and federal laws addressing minimum wage, overtime, and salary (for "exempt" employees). Some of these laws also address what information must be included on an employee's paystub.

- **When should an employee be paid?** How many days after an employee performs work is the employer required to pay the employee? This becomes particularly critical when the employment relationship ends.

- **When, and for how long, are employees entitled to breaks?** Several states have strict laws governing the provision of meal periods and rest breaks to nonexempt employees. These laws and regulations govern when breaks have to be provided (and the meaning of "provided" itself), the circumstances in which breaks can be waived by the employee, what constitutes a "duty-free" break, and the penalties that must be paid to employees when they are not provided a compliant break.

- **When can employees work, and who can work?** There is a large body of wage and hour law addressing questions about the types of schedules employers can implement, including schedules that permit employees to work hours that would usually be paid at overtime rates, but for special reasons do not qualify as overtime. There are also numerous laws about who can work, particularly laws regulating child labor.

- **What deductions can employers take from an employee's wages?** These laws and regulations concern when it is appropriate to deduct from an employee's paycheck for certain things like health care, retirement, personal loans, uniforms, or business losses caused by the employee.

- **Which wage and hour laws apply to which employees?** Some wage and hour laws only apply to employees in specific industries in specific states, while others apply broadly across the board. Within this framework under federal and state law there is a line drawn in the sand between exempt and nonexempt employees. There has been considerable litigation over the years on the question of whether an employer "misclassifies" certain employees as "exempt," which could make them entitled to overtime wages.

The questions above scratch the surface of the wage and hour universe. Maintaining compliant wage and hour practices requires considerable attention to detail and close collaboration between human resources, payroll, the business itself, and employment law attorneys. Managers do not need to be experts in wage and hour law. At the same time, those managers who regularly supervise nonexempt employees need to work on maintaining good wage and hour hygiene. The six lessons below are essential to this endeavor.

SIX WAGE & HOUR BEST PRACTICES EVERY MANAGER SHOULD EMBRACE

1. Understand Your Organization's Policies and Practices That Directly Impact Your Role as a Manager

Managers have enough on their plate that they do not have to develop, understand, and implement every wage and hour policy and practice within their organization. That is the job of HR and payroll. That said, effective managers do need to understand their role in ensuring that the organization has a culture of compliance around wage and hour issues. If you are not sure about your role in this regard, I recommend that you put the book down for a minute and send an email to your contact in HR, requesting a meeting or additional training on the specific wage and hour issues that *you* are responsible for when managing your employees.

2. Be on the Lookout for Potential Off-the-Clock Issues

Nonexempt employees generally must be paid for all hours worked. Managers should not have their nonexempt employees perform compensable work unless the employee is being paid for their time. The first rule of off-the-clock work is simple: a manager should never ask an employee who is off the clock to continue working with the understanding that they will not be paid for this time. If an employee is off the clock, and their manager needs them to take care of a work-related matter at that moment, the manager should first have the employee clock back in, or at least make sure the employee's records are adjusted to take the additional time worked into account. Going one step further, managers should be aware of instances within their unique work environment that could lead to off-the-clock issues. Consider the following examples:

- After a cook clocks out for the day, the restaurant manager notices that the cook is staying around the kitchen to clean up the work area and help prepare inventory for the following day. Once the manager is aware that this is happening, the manager needs to stop this practice. The manager should also consider whether the restaurant has an obligation to pay the cook for the time spent cleaning up and conducting inventory after clocking out for the day.

- An office worker who clocks out every day around 5:00 p.m. sends a work-related email at 7:00 p.m. at night. When you check the employee's time records, you determine that the employee clocked out that day at 5:02 p.m. You are now on notice that the employee worked off the clock. You need to consult with HR on what to do next, which may include paying the employee for that time, and counseling the employee on the prohibition of employees working off the clock and the importance of time-clock etiquette.

- An employee prefers to come into work an hour early to have a cup of coffee in the breakroom and get to their station in the factory 20 minutes before the assembly line bell rings. Even though the employee is not actually working, a conversation may be in order to remind the employee about when it is appropriate to first go to their station to avoid the potential of pre-shift off-the-clock work.

3. Meal and Rest Break Compliance

Federal wage and hour law, as codified in the Fair Labor Standards Act (FLSA) does not contain meal and rest-break requirements. Yet as previously discussed, many states have adopted specific requirements regarding the circumstances when an employee is entitled to take a paid rest break and an unpaid meal period. If you manage nonexempt employees in a state where meal and rest breaks are required, it is important to make sure you have a clear understanding of your company's policies. Because the financial penalties for noncompliance with the law in this area can be significant in some states, particularly in California, managers in states with meal and rest-break requirements often need to schedule their employees with these requirements in mind.

4. Clear All Bonus and Commission Plans with HR Before Rolling Them Out

Several wage and hour laws fall into the category of "no good deed goes unpunished." One in particular is giving employees more money in bonuses and commissions. Depending on the type of bonus and the nature of the commission, the money received by the employee on the bonus or commission can also impact the employee's overtime rate. Without getting too much into the weeds on this issue, it is a common misconception that the overtime rate for most employees is simply 1.5× or 2.0× the employee's hourly base rate. That is rarely the case. The overtime rate is actually 1.5× or 2.0× the employee's "regular rate of pay," which can be a bit higher than the employee's base rate. The regular rate of pay includes the employee's base wages earned during that measuring period *plus* certain nondiscretionary bonuses (such as attendance and production bonuses), commissions, and in some cases, even nonmonetary forms of compensation (e.g., certain meals, lodging, etc.). To avoid unwittingly getting sued for paying employees more money because a bonus or commission was not factored into the overtime rate, make sure to first clear the plan with HR before you decide to motivate your employees to be more productive, increase attendance, or sell more products.

5. Make a Record When Adjusting Time Punches

A month from now, let alone four years from now, you will not remember why on a random Tuesday you adjusted an employee's time records by changing a time-clock punch from 5:30 p.m. back to 5:15 p.m. Without an explanation for the adjustment, it may look like you intentionally deprived the employee of 15 minutes of pay. The real reason may be that the employee stopped working at 5:15, but didn't clock out until 5:30 and asked you to adjust their time record. Without documentation to prove that is what happened, however, years later the employee may claim that you made this adjustment for an illegitimate reason.

There are two general rules for managers who have the ability to adjust an employee's time records. First, only make an adjustment when it is warranted. Employees must be paid for the time they worked (as "time" and "worked" are both legal terms of art), and it is entirely unacceptable for a manager to improperly "shave off" an employee's time. Second, if a manager is going to make an adjustment to an employee's time records, make sure they document the reason for the adjustment. The best record is one where the employee asks for it in an email or acknowledges it in some other fashion. If that is not possible, then at the very least, the manager should note the reasons for the adjustment and maintain the record in a central file.

6. Encourage Employees to Bring Forward Wage and Hour Concerns

The single best thing a leader can do to avoid expensive wage and hour litigation is make it well known to employees that if they have any wage and hour concerns, they should bring them to the manager's attention so that the issues can be resolved without delay. I had a case years ago where the ex-employee claimed that he only received 75 percent of the commissions he was owed for three years. When I asked the ex-employee at his deposition whether he ever complained to his manager, he offered a rather lame explanation for his inaction: "My manager never told me that I should let him know if I had any payroll issues." Whether or not that is true, a leader who Manages Without Fear communicates to their employees that it is very important that they get paid accurately, for all the time they work, and in compliance with state and federal law. And furthermore, if any employee ever feels they are not being paid properly, the employee should immediately bring their concerns directly to their manager, HR, or the payroll department.

...

While it is important for a people manager to appreciate the public policies and history that have led to laws that prohibit discrimination and workplace harassment—as we have discussed in prior chapters—the same is not true for wage and hour laws. A leader need only understand *their role* in enforcing their organization's wage and hour policies and procedures. As long as a leader understands their role and maintains good wage and hour hygiene, they are satisfying their obligations to their employees and their employer.

MANAGING WITHOUT FEAR PLAYBOOK

Seven Lessons Every Leader Should Follow to Create a Culture of Compliance around Wage and Hour Laws

1. Leaders should understand their role and responsibilities with respect to the organization's wage and hour policies and procedures.

2. Absent unique exceptions, leaders should be vigilant in preventing their nonexempt/"hourly" employees from performing compensable "off-the-clock" work.

3. Leaders must be mindful of their organization's meal and rest-break requirements, particularly in those states that mandate statutory meal and rest breaks.

4. Before introducing any bonus or commission plans to nonexempt employees, even ones that seem relatively minor, receive permission from your organization's human resource and payroll professionals first.

5. Whenever a leader needs to adjust a nonexempt employee's time records, it is important to make a record documenting the reasons why the adjustment is necessary and legitimate.

6. Encourage employees to bring forward any wage and hour concerns or issues in a timely manner.

7. Leaders should bring any questions they have concerning wage and hour compliance to their human resource business partner. Recognizing that wage and hour laws are complicated, and noncompliance can pose significant risks to an organization, is the hallmark of a leader who manages without fear.

CHAPTER 14

Managing Remote Workers

March 19, 2020, may very well go down in history as the day that *how* and *where* millions of Americans work changed forever. On that day, in an early effort to "flatten the curve" and stop the COVID-19 infection rate, California Governor Gavin Newsom ordered every Californian who was not deemed an "essential worker" to stay at home. In the years leading up to the pandemic, employers were beginning to become more comfortable with the idea of flexible work arrangements. The confluence of rapid advances in communication technology, a tight labor market, and the rise of millennial employees who demand greater work/life balance, forced many companies to accept flexible work arrangements, often begrudgingly. Then came the COVID-19 pandemic. By the end of March 2020, the coronavirus forced nearly every employer in the country and tens of millions of employees to fully transition from working in an office to working at their kitchen tables—something that had previously been considered a novelty for many employers. When the dust finally settles on the COVID-19 chapter, one of the lasting impacts will likely be a drastic transformation in how and where many employees work. Managers will be expected to adapt to this new way of leading their teams.

Successfully managing a remote workforce creates unique challenges for managers, particularly around employment law compliance issues. Fortunately, all of the lessons from the previous chapters apply regardless of whether an employee works 10 feet from your desk or 500 miles from your home office. The key difference is that when managing a remote workforce, leaders need to be especially sensitive to a number of issues and how they translate from an office environment to a remote environment.

NURTURING A PSYCHOLOGICALLY SAFE CULTURE MATTERS EVEN MORE IN A WORK-FROM-HOME UNIVERSE

In 2012, Google launched an internal study—code name Project Aristotle—to figure out the reason why some business teams thrive while others flounder. The investigators had Google employees on 180 teams complete elaborate questionnaires, asking everything from whether employees socialize with other members of their team outside of the office, to whether employees preferred to work with extroverts or introverts. The investigators were initially frustrated because they could not discern any noticeable patterns. Whether or not team members spent time together outside of work had no bearing on the team's success. Nor was there any correlation between teams with a clear hierarchal structure compared to those with a more egalitarian organization. They soon realized that hidden in the answers were details about each team's social norms—the unwritten rules about how the team operates. The norms that a group has developed, often directed by the manager, establish the team's unique culture. Yes, every work group has norms that members of the group understand, but which norms lead to the most productive teams? After further rigorous analysis, the investigators on Project Aristotle uncovered one team norm that stood well above all others in separating successful teams from mediocre ones: psychological safety.

According to Professor Amy Edmondson of Harvard Business School and author of *The Fearless Organization: Creating Psychological Safety in the Workplace for Learning, Innovation, and Growth*, psychological safety "describes a team climate characterized by interpersonal trust and mutual respect in which people are comfortable being themselves." A psychologically safe team is one where members feel comfortable asking for help, admitting their shortcomings, and voicing dissenting ideas. The team forms a bond around interpersonal trust and mutual respect for each other's differences. So much of creating a work environment that promotes diversity and inclusion, as we discussed in Chapter 10, centers around the idea that when employees feel psychologically safe at work, they tend to be more productive, more loyal to the organization, and more invested in their work and the team's overall success. Psychological safety is an essential element of the most successful business organizations. Unfortunately, it is also a social norm that does not easily translate to a remote working environment.

Managers who recognize the importance of promoting psychologically safe teams need to be much more intentional about fostering this social norm when they have remote workers. In an office environment, there are plenty of informal opportunities for employees to get to know and learn from one another, and the environment tends to be more conducive to having conversations that create a safe space to learn from one's mistakes. Remote working does not naturally lend itself to fostering these opportunities. This is especially acute when much of the team's communication is dominated by email or group chats—a medium that lacks the nuances of nonverbal communication. While video conference technologies can help teams create interpersonal relationships in a remote environment, staring at people's faces on a computer screen for hours on end is far from ideal, and it is not a substitute for in-person communications. Creating opportunities for remote workers to foster a psychologically safe environment, particularly where teams have a mix of in-office and remote employees, is difficult but certainly doable.

CONSTANT AND QUALITY FEEDBACK IS EVEN MORE IMPORTANT IN A REMOTE WORLD

Recall that in Chapter 7 we discussed the importance of regular feedback, and that employees generally prefer constructive criticism that shows their manager is invested in their career development, over generic positive reviews. Also remember that it is not always easy for managers to give constructive criticism. One solution to this problem is adopting the 1+1 method. To recap, when managers provide quick day-to-day feedback to their employees, it is useful to offer one thing to praise the employee and one piece of constructive criticism.

In a remote work environment, focusing on the feedback loop shows employees that their manager is closely and thoughtfully monitoring their work. It also creates a record of where the employee needs to improve. As discussed earlier, regular documentation helps leaders avoid falling into implicit bias traps when it comes time to draft formal employee reviews. While your remote worker may be out of sight, a robust feedback loop tells them they are not out of mind.

ESTABLISH CLEAR EXPECTATIONS

One of the biggest challenges when managing remote workers is developing clear expectations about the employee's availability and schedule. I have found that the remote working relationship most often breaks down when managers feel their employees are not focused on their work responsibilities—especially when the employee is unavailable at a time the manager needs or expects them to be available. If an employee is working remotely to balance childcare responsibilities, it is entirely appropriate for the manager to set expectations as to when the employee must be available. Putting aside wage and hour concerns for nonexempt employees, as discussed below, it is reasonable to work with an employee to create a customized schedule unless the job requires that the employee be at their computer during the entire workday and provided the company's culture is amenable to flexible schedules. A flexible schedule may mean the employee works earlier in the morning, later in the evening, or on weekends so that they can be offline during portions of the traditional workday to focus on childcare needs or personal pursuits. While flexible work hours is an option, it is generally reasonable for the manager to invite a discussion with a remote employee to determine a realistic work schedule that meets the company's needs while providing the employee some of the flexibility they desire. It is ultimately the employer who decides whether to give an employee their requested schedule. Absent a potential disability accommodation issue, employers are not legally required to provide flexible work arrangements. In many instances, however, providing greater flexibility for remote employees is an important component of a company's retention efforts, especially in recruiting and retaining female employees who are statistically overwhelmingly responsible for the lion's share of childcare responsibilities.

WAGE AND HOUR CONCERNS

Work-from-home arrangements raise a host of wage and hour compliance issues. As discussed in Chapter 13, nonexempt employees must be paid for all hours worked with the exception in most states of legally *de minimis* time. In an in-office environment, managers have more opportunities to monitor employee wage and hour compliance. In a work-from-home situation, non-exempt employees need to develop similar routines to avoid off-the-clock issues. The key takeaway for a manager is that generally the wage and hour protocols that exist in an in-person office environment must translate to a work-from-home situation. Before managers deviate from an established wage and hour policy, whether to accommodate an employee's schedule or because the employee lives in a different state, the manager should first raise the issue with HR or their own supervisor.

DATA SECURITY AND PRIVACY

Allowing employees to work remotely creates additional risks around data security and privacy concerns. Generally speaking, a frontline manager should not be responsible for establishing these policies. Nor should a manager try to "MacGyver" their own practices to monitor their employees during the workday, such as installing spy programs to monitor keystrokes or secretly observe employees while they are sitting in their home office. Managers should, however, bring any concerns relating to data privacy and security for their remote workers to the appropriate leaders within their organization.

...

Time will tell whether remote working arrangements truly become the next frontier of the American workplace. If it turns out that in the wake of the COVID-19 pandemic a large percentage of workers regularly work from home, it will forever change how managers lead teams spread across multiple time zones and countries. While I am not prepared to declare that the traditional office environment is on a trajectory to become an endangered species, leaders have to be prepared to effectively and legally adapt their management style and practice to the virtual office.

• • • • • • • • • • •

MANAGING WITHOUT FEAR PLAYBOOK

Best Practices When Managing Remote Workers

1. Leaders must be even more mindful of the importance of nurturing a psychologically safe culture for their employees who work from home.

2. Providing employees with regular and quality feedback is even more imperative when employees and their managers work in different locations.

3. Establish clear and measurable performance expectations, particularly when an employee works a flexible schedule to balance their personal childcare or other responsibilities with their work duties.

4. Remember that virtually all of the wage and hour requirements that exist for employees working in an office also exist for employees working from home.

5. Leaders and their organizations should be particularly mindful of the data privacy and security issues that are unique to employees who primarily or exclusively work from home.

CHAPTER 15

It's So Hard to Say Goodbye

Surviving Resignations, Layoffs, and Involuntary Separations

In the 2009 movie *Up In the Air,* downsizing consultant Ryan Bingham, played by George Clooney, traverses the country while amassing millions of frequent flyer miles. His job, according to the Hollywoodized version of corporate America, is to do what managers apparently are too scared to do: fire their employees. Clooney's character is paired with a savvy younger consultant, Natalie Keener, played expertly by Anna Kendrick. She convinces the company that its future lies in having termination meetings via video conference. Bingham despises this idea, albeit primarily for selfish reasons. Going virtual will deprive him of his nomadic lifestyle and quest for the elusive 10 million frequent flier miles. He also questions the premise of firing employees on video—which, in his mind, is somehow less honorable than hiring a stranger to deliver the bad news. The film ultimately weaves together the emotions one feels at the loss of a job with similar emotions of a broken heart (I am intentionally avoiding the big spoiler if you have not seen the movie). The film's lasting message is that efforts to try and scrub human emotion from work and romantic breakups is naïve. Giving another human bad news in person with compassion and empathy is often neither easy nor efficient, but is usually the right thing to do.

It is not uncommon in the HR and employment law world to hear analogies between stages in the employee-employer relationship and lifecycle events. Pregnancy equates to recruiting new employees. Birth somehow pairs with hiring. Early childhood is like onboarding new employees. Adolescence is analogous with training employees and helping them assimilate into the company's culture. Adulthood is employees growing, taking on even greater responsibilities, and perhaps being promoted. And then it ends with either a divorce (when employees resign and move to a new job) or, hyperbole aside, death (when an employer "terminates" an employee or offers retirement after a long productive tenure). The lifecycle/employment analogy is imperfect, insensitive, and rather silly (particularly the idea that hiring and training employees is anything like raising a child). I see it more along the lines of how Walter Kirn—the author of the novel on which *Up in the Air* is based—allegorized life in general: a lengthy flight. And like every long-haul flight, the ultimate goal is to land the plane safely at its final destination, wherever that may be.

At this, the penultimate chapter, we address how to bring the employment relationship to a "safe" landing. Ending the employment relationship, whether for performance reasons, because of a layoff, or due to a resignation, can be fraught with problems. A leader who manages without fear is well aware of the risks if they fail to "stick the landing." This leader is also confident that because they have treated their employees fairly and legally, they have put their organization in the best position to end the relationship without unnecessary drama, and hopefully without litigation.

TERMINATIONS, LAYOFFS, AND RESIGNATIONS: SIMILARITIES AND DIFFERENCES

There are three principal ways an employment relationship ends: involuntary terminations, layoffs, and resignations.

An involuntary termination is where the employer makes the decision to end the employment relationship for performance reasons (the relationship is being terminated, not the employee). Where the employment relationship is "at-will," the employer does not need to have a reason to let an employee go—that is, as long as the reason is not unlawful. As discussed in previous chapters, the subtle erosion of the very concept of the at-will employment relationship in the United States (or at least as it is applied to the employer severing the relationship) usually means that the employer should be able to demonstrate a legitimate reason for its decision. Documenting the reasons therefore becomes essential in establishing that the separation was based on legitimate nondiscriminatory and nonretaliatory reasons.

Involuntarily separating an employee who is under contract with the employer imposes a heightened standard on the employer. Employees who are members of a union that has negotiated a collective bargaining agreement directly with the employer typically have layers of job security. Most collective bargaining agreements, and many employment contracts, impose a "for cause" test for the employer to involuntarily separate an employee. The types of behaviors that can constitute "cause" are usually spelled out in the employment contract. Managers who supervise employees in a union environment, or in an organization that has strict progressive discipline policies, must be aware of these requirements before making any termination decisions.

Layoffs are also involuntary separations—however the employee is being let go, not for individual performance reasons, but for business reasons. Corporate downsizings, reorganizations, store closures, and changed business circumstances often result in companies being forced to make the difficult decision to reduce headcount.

Finally an employee can obviously quit their job. Usually the parting is amicable, with leadership wishing the employee good luck on their next opportunity—or in my analogy, their next flight. There are nevertheless a number of red flags a manager should be on the lookout for when an employee resigns.

Whether the separation is voluntary or involuntary, there are three common components to help achieve a "safe" landing.

Have a Communication Plan in Place

Without an employee giving notice and immediately walking out the door, there is usually enough time for leadership to formulate a plan to communicate the decision to the departing employee (in the case of an involuntary separation) and the team. For involuntary terminations, the first rung of the plan usually requires careful consideration of who will lead the conversation and what will be communicated to the employee regarding the reasons why the employee is being let go.

Some organizations have very specific protocols in place concerning who is in the room, where everyone sits (e.g., the employee being let go should always be closest to the door), and what is communicated to the employee. Other organizations expect HR to take the lead in any conversation, with the employee's manager in a supportive role. Still others maintain ad hoc processes. Whatever the procedure is, it is important that managers know what is expected of them during these meetings before communicating the decision. In addition to logistical concerns (e.g., COBRA paperwork, final paychecks, etc.), everyone going into the meeting should be prepared to respond to the three questions that most often come up when an employee is being given bad news:

1. "I would like to know the reasons why you are letting me go?"
2. "Why are you firing me and not _____?"
3. "Are you going to offer me a severance or some other type of support?"

The second rung of communications focuses on internal stakeholders. How is leadership going to communicate this decision to other employees within the organization? This often requires a delicate balance of (1) respecting the departing employee's privacy, (2) quashing rumors about why the employee was separated, (3) reassuring the team that their jobs are secure, which is especially important after a layoff, and (4) describing the plan going forward on how work will be distributed across the team. When communicating why an employee has been involuntarily separated, less is usually more. When approached about why an employee on your team is leaving the company, the best response is usually the simplest: "This is a private personnel matter and I am not at liberty to discuss it." Another common response, and one that is even more vague, is simply: "_____ has left our organization, and we wish _____ the best of luck going forward."

Finally, if the employee is customer or client facing, or has regular business contacts with folks outside of the organization, there should be a plan on how to communicate the personnel decision to external stakeholders. Similar to the internal audience, the outward-bound message generally should be positive and reassuring that the employee's departure will not cause any business interruptions. Having a forward-looking concrete plan is key to assuaging any concerns from customers or clients that their needs will go unmet because the departing employee is no longer with the organization.

Post-Employment Obligations: Noncompete Agreements and Trade Secrets

There are three stages to the employee relationship: pre-employment, employment, and post-employment. Up to now, we have only focused on the first two.

The ending of the formal employment relationship usually does not mean the end of the relationship. Saying goodbye (or good riddance) to an employee is often coupled with a reminder of the employee's post-employment obligations. It is very likely that you, and all of your employees, are contractually bound to a number of requirements concerning confidentiality and trade secrets. And even if you are not, federal and state laws prohibit current and former employees from misappropriating trade secrets and confidential information to benefit another employer. In addition, depending on the state where you work, you and some of your employees may also be subject to post-employment "noncompete" agreements or "restrictive covenants" limiting where you can work, the ability to solicit specific customers/clients, and the ability to solicit employees to join a new company.

The law governing post-employment restrictions and misappropriation of trade secrets and confidential information is complicated. Managers should "stick to the script" from HR or in-house legal counsel when discussing any post-employment obligations with a departing employee. If the employee is subject to enforceable noncompete and/or nonsolicitation agreements, it is advisable to provide the employee with a copy of these agreements upon the employee's exit. It is also a good idea to have a very frank and serious conversation about the employee's obligation to protect the organization's trade secrets and confidential information. At the same time, if a leader has *any* reason to suspect a departing employee (often but not always when an employee is resigning) has taken confidential information (e.g., emailing themselves customer lists, copying confidential business plans, etc.), the manager should immediately bring their concerns to the attention of HR, in-house legal, or their direct supervisor.

Exit Plan

Every employee departure should include a clear exit plan. The reason why the employee is leaving, and whether it is voluntary or involuntary, often dictates the exit plan. This is the action plan formalizing the commitments made to internal and external stakeholders. It also makes sure that the departing employee has returned all company property, is paid final wages (some states require final payment of wages at separation), and understands their post-employment obligations. In the event that there are concerns that the employee may react to the news of their separation in a hostile manner, the exit plan may also require having security available to escort the employee out of the workplace. If there is a concern that the employee is walking out the door with the company's trade secrets, the plan may also include hiring a computer forensic expert to examine the employee's computer and work cell phone.

INVOLUNTARY SEPARATION

For obvious reasons, involuntary separations for performance reasons tend to be a hot zone for employment litigation. Decisions leading up to separating an employee for performance reasons (regardless of whether the employment relationship is at-will or not) are among the most scrutinized decisions managers make. A manager without fear knows this well, and has made a string of decisions up to that point in accordance with the organization's policies and the law. As is often the case, however, even if leadership and HR have maintained a culture of compliance in the workplace and consistently coached and documented the employee's poor performance, this decision could very well be put under a microscope and picked apart for years to come in litigation. Before arriving at the ultimate decision to separate the employee, the decision maker should be able to provide cogent answers to the following seven important questions.

Seven Questions to Consider Before Terminating an Underperforming Employee

1. Are we separating the employee for the same (or very similar) transgression committed by a different employee who was not separated?

A version of the following phone conversation takes place every day across the country between a recently separated employee and an attorney the ex-employee wants to hire to sue their former employer:

Ex-employee: I believe my employer discriminated or retaliated against me, and I want to file a lawsuit.

Attorney: That is a serious accusation. Why do you think you were discriminated or retaliated against?"

Ex-employee: Well. . . let me think. When my manager told me that the company would be letting me go, he said that it was due to "performance reasons." When I asked him what reasons, he said that I had _____ [*fill in the reason*].

Attorney: Okay, well did you in fact do _____ [*reason*]?

Ex-employee: Well. . . yes, I did do that. But other employees have done the same thing, and they were only written up, where I was immediately fired.

Attorney: You may have a case. Let's find a time to meet to review your allegations. Please be sure to bring every disciplinary write-up and performance evaluation you have with you to our meeting.

Recall that employment discrimination is the unequal treatment of an employee due to the employee's membership in a "protected class," and retaliation is punishing an employee for engaging in "protected activity." One way this can manifest itself is when an employer separates an employee for a transgression that other employees—namely, other employees who are not in the protected class or who have not engaged in protected activity—do not receive such a severe punishment for. Certainly there may be legitimate reasons to separate an employee for a transgression when another employee may only receive a write-up. For example, the separated employee may have been previously admonished for this behavior, while the other employee had not. Or maybe this is but one of a series of transgressions that, when placed into context, explains why one employee is exited from the organization while another may only receive a suspension. The important lesson here, as echoed throughout the book, is that if an employer is going to separate an employee for violating a specific policy or other performance reasons, and has not (or would not in the future) necessarily terminate another employee at that same level for the same wrongdoing, there should be documentation in the departing employee's file clearly explaining the legitimacy of the employer's reasons.

2. If we have a progressive discipline policy, are we following it? If not, why not?

In Chapter 8, we discussed how to legally discipline employees. One of the eight identified strategies is the importance of fastidiously abiding by the organization's policies, including any applicable "progressive discipline" policies. Before making the final separation decision, it is important to take a step back and ask whether the decision follows the next step of the progressive discipline ladder, and if not, whether there is a legitimate justification to jump over stages and go straight to separation. If there are concerns that the termination decision bypasses established company discipline protocols, it is wise to slow things down and consider another disciplinary action.

3. Why not consider additional discipline, including possibly a "Performance Improvement Plan" or a demotion?

Recruiting, hiring, training, coaching, and managing a single employee is a considerable investment for every organization. Before deciding to pull the plug on the employment relationship due to performance reasons, it is worthwhile to at least ask whether it makes sense to separate the employee without at least exploring other disciplinary actions. The answer may very well be that the nature of the employee's misconduct does not warrant a second chance, or that the organization has already provided numerous opportunities for the employee to improve their performance. At the very least, however, there should be a discussion as to whether an alternative to separation is worth considering.

4. If you are separating the employee for violating a company policy, is it written, was the employee aware of the policy, and does the employee have a legitimate excuse for violating the policy?

Before deciding to move forward with a separation because an employee violated a company policy, it is important to ask whether there is, in fact, a policy that the employee violated. Not every policy must be in writing or formalized in an employee handbook or manual (although it is certainly a best practice to do so). Concerns can arise when a manager cites a "policy violation" and there is scant evidence that such a policy exists. As a leader, if you are in a position to recommend separating an employee for a specific policy violation, you should be able to cite the policy, explain how it was violated, and confirm that other employees have or would be separated for a similar violation—unless, of course, this violation was the proverbial last straw.

Managers should also be on the lookout for an employee's *legitimate* excuse for violating a policy. This is where a quality investigation can prevent a costly mistake. Say, for example, that the reason for the separation is a history of chronic tardiness. This would be as legitimate a reason as any to separate an employee. But what if the employee had reached an agreement with their former supervisor that, for childcare reasons, they could start work 30 minutes late every Tuesday and Thursday? And what if the employee's new manager or HR is unaware of this arrangement, leading to the conclusion that the employee took advantage of a lax supervisor? These could all be legitimate reasons for why the employee's time records show a consistent pattern of tardiness. A quick investigation would uncover that this employee had permission to start work late twice a week, even if the former supervisor who gave the employee permission did not have the authority to make this accommodation. On occasion, an employee may have an entirely legitimate reason or excuse for a policy violation. Giving an employee the opportunity to explain why they believe their violation should be excused is a fair and efficient way to avoid a potential wrongful termination.

5. Has the employee made a compliant within the last 6 to 12 months that *could* give rise to a retaliation claim?

Sadly, it is not uncommon for employees heading toward separation for performance reasons to make "compliance" or "whistleblower" complaints in an effort to salvage their jobs. Knowing that a well-timed complaint of questionable veracity can disrupt personnel decisions, I have seen far too many employees try to manufacture retaliation claims. Just because an employee lodges a complaint does not magically grant them immunity. It usually does, however, require that the employer be able to demonstrate that an adverse personnel decision (e.g., a write-up, demotion, or separation) was not made in retaliation for the compliant. The best way to avoid an accusation that a leader's decision was pretextual is by having ample documentation to support the decision to separate the employee. Incorporating the lessons from earlier chapters is the best way to establish the legitimacy of the employer's actions.

While fabricated complaints are sadly common, employees of course should, and do, bring forward legitimate complaints and concerns. A strong manager encourages their employees to appropriately shine a spotlight on such concerns without fear of retaliation. A strong manager is also on the lookout for other leaders within their organization who may, for personal reasons, make adverse employment decisions to punish employees for making complaints. Just as bringing forward an illegitimate complaint does not give an employee immunity, neither does a valid complaint. In both situations, the employer must be able to show that the personnel decision was not made for retaliatory reasons. As a best practice, if an employee has filed a complaint within the last 12 months, it is wise to look at any separation decision through the lens of retaliation law. If there is even a hint that a manager along the decision-making chain *may* have a retaliatory motive, it is worth consulting with in-house or outside counsel.

6. Should you consider offering a severance agreement to the departing employee?

A severance agreement is a contract between the departing employee and the employer where the employer agrees to pay the employee a sum of money (the severance amount) in exchange for the employee agreeing not to sue the employer, often along with a variety of other terms (e.g., confidentiality, nondisparagement, etc.). The decision on whether to offer employees a severance is usually made at the highest levels of an organization. Some organizations have a clear-cut rule that they never offer severance to an employee who is being separated for performance reasons. Others strongly encourage severance agreements, having adopted formulas for how much money to pay a departing employee based on objective factors such as years of service or position within the organization. Still others take a cautious individualized approach toward severance decisions.

The decision to offer an employee a voluntary severance package, like the decision to settle an employment lawsuit, is not an admission by the employer that they mistreated the departing employee or did anything wrong. It is more about tying up loose ends. I would never suggest that employers should always, or even usually, offer severance to employees being separated for performance reasons. Provided the organization is generally amenable to such arrangements, however, it is worthwhile for the manager to have a conversation with their HR partner about whether it makes sense in a particular situation. Because severance agreements are usually confidential documents, prepared by experienced employment counsel, a frontline manager should not be surprised if the ultimate decision is made by HR in consultation with in-house or outside counsel.

7. If you are asked two years from now in a lawsuit to justify why you made the termination decision, how will you respond?

When managers make the decision to part ways with an employee, it is important that they be able to articulate, in no more than a few sentences, the reason(s) for the decision. If the explanation appears to be too convoluted or too vague, leaders should go back to the drawing board. When asked by HR why they want to separate an employee, leaders must be able to muster more than "it just did not work out." If leaders cannot clearly articulate their reasons at the time the decision is made, it will be difficult to summon the reasons for the decision years later in the course of litigation.

LAYOFFS

As mentioned, a layoff is an involuntary termination due to business reasons that are not directly related to the poor performance of the employee being let go. Typically, when an organization has to make a layoff or reduction in force, the decisions are made at higher levels of the organization in consultation with HR and legal counsel. Far from spectators, however, frontline people managers have a role in making sure layoffs are done fairly and with an eye toward making sure employee morale does not suffer. There are two main legal concerns employers should consider before conducting a mass layoff due to a downturn in the business or a corporate restructuring.

Disparate Impact Considerations

As you recall from Chapter 10, employers must be mindful that their decisions do not have a disparate discriminatory impact on certain classes of employees. Consider the following scenario. A company just experienced three negative quarters and the CEO needs to reduce headcount to prevent financial calamity. After running the numbers, the CEO tells every manager they must reduce headcount on their teams by 25 percent. The CEO leaves it up to each manager to select the employees that will be part of the layoff, reminding managers of their obligation to abide by the company's EEO policy and commitment to diversity and inclusion. Each manager then submits their list of employees selected for the reduction in force.

One of HR's responsibilities is to make sure that the layoff does not raise any disparate impact concerns. First, HR pulls the demographics of the workforce and calculates that of the company's 400 employees considered for the layoff, 40 percent are women, 20 percent are employees of color, and 38 percent are over the age of 40. HR then pulls the list of the 100 employees targeted for layoffs, and calculates that 45 of them are women, 10 are employees of color, and 60 are over 40 years of age (several employees check multiple boxes). Are there any concerns that this layoff may have a disparate impact on any employees in a protected class? Women make up a slightly higher portion of employees subject to the layoff, but probably not a statistically significant one. No issues with employees of color. That leaves "older" employees (i.e., employees over the age of 40). Although this group only makes up 38 percent of the workforce, they currently make up 60 percent of the employees who will be hit by the layoff. Without legitimate reasons, as discussed below, the layoff may unintentionally have a disparate impact on older workers.

In this scenario, the CEO should have provided managers with better direction on how to select employees for layoffs. There is not a one-size-fits-all approach to setting criteria for reductions in force, nor is there a common method to weighing different criteria. Employers may opt for objective metrics such as seniority (i.e., "last to hire, first to fire") or sales performance. Employers may instead also use more subjective tests, including performance ratings and decisions based on retaining employees with specific skill sets. Due to the complexities associated with analyzing reductions in force, it is sometimes necessary to bring in employment law experts to ensure that the layoff does not violate federal and/or state discrimination laws.

WARN Considerations

Under specific circumstances, the federal Worker Adjustment and Retraining Notification (WARN) Act, along with state mini-WARN Acts, require employers to provide 60 days advance notice to employees who will be impacted by a plant closing or mass layoffs of 50 or more employees. These laws are particularly complex. It is another area of employment law that a manager should not try to navigate without support from experienced HR and employment law experts. I only bring it up here to highlight how a mass layoff can trigger federal and state notice requirements, and that the failure to abide by WARN laws can result in considerable penalties.

RESIGNATIONS

Other than the preliminary considerations discussed earlier in this chapter applicable to involuntary separations, resignations typically do not implicate any additional employment law concerns. The only exception to this is if the employee takes the position at the time of resignation (or sometimes months later) that they were "forced" to resign due to a discriminatory, retaliatory, or hostile work environment. In employment law speak, this is referred to as a "constructive termination" theory. The key here is that sometimes employees resign because they believe, rightly or wrongly, that they could not continue working in that environment. The best way to determine whether an employee is resigning to avoid being subjected to mistreatment by another employee is by asking the employee to participate in an exit interview.

Exit interviews are an excellent opportunity for an organization to determine why an employee is leaving. If large numbers of employees are resigning because they are getting better offers from a competitor, that may prompt senior management to increase compensation. If employers learn that employees in a particular department are leaving *en masse*, there may be an issue with the head of that department's management style. Exit interviews also provide employers an opportunity for a candid discussion of the workplace, particularly around employment law compliance issues. At the very least, I encourage employers to ask (and document) the following six questions, along with necessary follow-up, during an exit interview, all of which touch upon employment law issues:

1. What prompted you to look for a new job?
2. How would you describe our company's work culture?
3. During your employment, was there ever a time where you made a complaint about an issue in the workplace that you believe was not taken seriously or not properly investigated by your manager or HR?
4. Do you have any complaints or concerns that you would like to bring to the attention of leadership about your experiences working for our organization?
5. Would you ever consider returning to this organization in the future?
6. Would you recommend working here to your friends and family?

There is no need to sugarcoat it: letting employees go or accepting resignations is among the least desirable parts of a people manager's job. Yet unlike the faceless managers in the movie *Up In The Air*, who contracted with George Clooney's character to perform this task, a manager without fear does not approach this with consternation or trepidation, as they are confident they are making a decision that is best for the organization and fully in compliance with the law.

• • • • • • • • • • •
MANAGING WITHOUT FEAR PLAYBOOK

Seven Key Considerations When Involuntarily Separating an Employee for Performance Reasons

1. Determine whether the employee is being separated for the same, or very similar, transgressions committed by another employee who was not separated. In the event this occurs, confirm that the separation decision is not influenced by potential discriminatory or retaliatory reasons.

2. If the organization has a "progressive discipline" policy or practice, confirm that it is being followed, and if not, ensure there are legitimate nondiscriminatory and nonretaliatory reasons for deviating from the policy/practice.

3. Before making the final separation decision, determine whether it is prudent to put the employee on a performance improvement plan, demote the employee, or issue some other disciplinary action short of separation.

4. When separating an employee for violating a company policy, first confirm whether the policy is written. Then ask whether other employees under similar circumstances have/would also be separated. Finally, determine whether the employee has a legitimate excuse for violating the policy.

5. Be mindful of potential retaliation claims. If the employee has made a complaint in the last 6 to 12 months, confirm that the decision to separate the employee is not related to any potential retaliatory reasons.

6. Work with the human resources department to determine whether it is appropriate to offer the employee a severance agreement.

7. Even though an employer does not technically need a reason to separate an "at-will" employee for performance reasons, it is important that the leader who makes the ultimate decision is able to articulate a clear and lawful explanation.

CHAPTER 16

A Few Parting Words

Having now completed this book, it is important to once again ask: what type of manager are you? My hope is that you can confidently answer that you are a manager who leads without fear. The time you invested in this book and finding ways to incorporate these lessons into your daily practice will pay dividends for years to come. As a proactive leader who cares deeply about fostering a culture of compliance within your organization, you are now in a position to model best practices to your fellow leaders and team members. Making personnel decisions from a place of knowledge and with a solid understanding of the employment law landscape, your employees will intuitively trust the bona fides of your decision, even if they do not necessarily agree with them. This is the power of managing without fear.

Now that you have mastered key principles of employment law, it is important you remain sharp and continue to hone your craft. There are several ways to do this. When given the opportunity, you should attend manager training offered by HR and outside experts. You can also subscribe to employment law blogs, including the Labor and Employment Law Blog hosted by my law firm, Sheppard Mullin, which can be found at www.laboremploymentlawblog.com, and the blog written by the publisher of this book, the Society for Human Resource Management (SHRM) at www.blog.shrm.org.

The best way for you to keep employment law compliance top of mind is by regularly working with the HR leaders within your organization. I have had the good fortune throughout my career to work with, learn from, and become friends with hundreds of HR professionals. The vast majority of HR leaders go into this field because they care deeply about people and want to partner with other leaders to create a workplace built on a strong foundation of legal compliance. I have also found that, not surprisingly, HR professionals tend to be superb listeners. When faced with a tricky personnel issue or a complicated decision, HR can be a trusted partner. Hopefully after reading this book, your employment law sonar is so finely tuned that you can identify potential issues well before they ever become serious problems. Involving HR early to help you better navigate these waters is the not-so-secret ingredient of the Managing Without Fear philosophy.

I would like to thank you for allowing me to be your tour guide on this journey. I appreciate that people managers tend to be expert jugglers—responsible for a host of important tasks in an effort to smoothly run their organization, and only one of them actually involves the management of people. Recognizing this, the fact that you are keenly aware of the central role you play in fostering a culture of compliance around employment law is particularly impressive. I decided to specialize in employment law early in my career, in large part because of the special relationship between an organization and their employment counsel. It's true that I am regularly called upon to defend my clients in contentious lawsuits. While I happen to enjoy the adversarial nature of litigation, and savor the opportunity to tell my client's story in front of a judge and jury, the aspect of my job that I enjoy the most is helping clients enact policies and practices to *avoid* litigation. I especially enjoy meeting with and training managers across the country on many of the topics covered in this book. To that end, if your organization would like to schedule a personalized manager employment law training session hosted by me or one of my colleagues, feel free to have your HR leaders or in-house attorneys reach out to me.

A final thought. Whether you are a first-time manager or have been doing this for decades, it is important to be mindful that the Managing Without Fear philosophy is premised on the notion that leaders are not expected or required to be infallible. We are only humans, of course. It is inevitable that you will say or do something at work that you will regret later, make a bad hire, or fumble the opportunity to discipline an employee. Unless the mistake is particularly egregious, it can usually be quickly rectified. The important thing is to reflect on these missteps, learn from them, and perform better the next time around. Making a concerted effort to build on your mistakes and celebrate successes is the mark of a true professional and the sign of a leader who manages without fear.

Afterword

The two most difficult extracurricular challenges I have set for myself are running a marathon and writing this book. Both required training, focus, and, in some measure, working through pain and exhaustion. The only reason I was able to accomplish both relatively unscathed is because I had the good fortune of being supported every step of the way by my best friend, soulmate, and wife, Jami. When I told Jami that "I absolutely needed" to write this book, it would have been entirely understandable if she had recommended that I put this project on hold until our three children were older, or wait until I could carve out a few months to focus exclusively on this project. But that is not what she said. She got fully behind me. On our nearly daily jogs through the neighborhood, Jami has been a sounding board as I worked my way through each chapter. Despite being at the helm of a busy house, embarking on a second career in marriage and family therapy, and remarkably having the bandwidth to be an extraordinary mother, wife, sister, daughter, friend, and employee, she also found the time to carefully read and critique the manuscript. This book could not have been written without Jami's support, encouragement, and love.

Staying with the marathon analogy for a moment, I am also forever grateful for our children, Ari, Talia, and Noah, who held up metaphorical signs of encouragement at every stage along the route of this project. I am in awe watching them discover and develop ways to make the world a more just, inclusive, and tolerant place. Seeing them grow up, I am supremely confident that their generation will finally solve many of the systemic societal problems that have flummoxed prior generations.

The most important lesson I impart on every law student and new attorney entering the profession is that the best way to achieve happiness and success as an attorney is by finding a few good mentors. Throughout my life, I have been especially fortunate in this regard. Without the risk of leaving anyone off, I am thankful for my mentors as an undergraduate at UCLA: Dr. Berky Nelson (may his memory be a blessing), Professor David Myers, and Rabbi Chaim Seidler-Feller. While in law school, I was fortunate to see the inner workings of the University of California system as a student member of the Board of Regents. In that role, I had the good fortune of being mentored by former Dean of the UC Davis School of Law, Rex R. Perschbacher (may his memory be a blessing), University of California President Robert Dynes, and UC Regents Sherry Lansing, Gerald Parsky, Peter Preuss, and Norm Pattiz.

As an attorney, I have had many mentors along the way. Two in particular stand out. Nancy Pritikin went from being my boss to later becoming my law partner. Yet despite our titles, she has always been my life coach, dear friend, and teacher. Many of the lessons and best practices in this book grew out of conversations we have had over more than a decade of working together. The entire legal profession, and I personally, owe a tremendous debt of gratitude to Nancy. Along with Nancy, I have had the good fortune to learn at the feet of a true master, John Adler—a brilliant attorney and all-around mensch. John has that rare ability to translate complex legal issues into practical "real world" advice. At every step of the way in this book, I made sure to listen to my "inner John" and asked myself how he would approach each subject.

I would not have been able to turn this book from an idea into a finished product without the unwavering support I have received from my colleagues at Sheppard, Mullin, Richter & Hampton LLP—the most brilliant and collegial cadre of attorneys on the planet. Moving to Sheppard Mullin in 2016 was by far the best professional decision I have ever made. I wish to express tremendous gratitude to our longtime Chairman Guy Halgren—an accomplished and courageous leader and mentor. I am also indebted to Larry Braun for his support and guidance throughout this process, and a constant reminder of how to create an inclusive workplace that is unapologetically committed to putting our clients first. In late March of 2020, as I was slogging my way through this manuscript, and just as the world was thrown into chaos by the COVID-19 pandemic, I received a call from my law partner Richard Simmons. In addition to being the world's most ardent Los Angeles Lakers fan, Richard is one of the most accomplished employment attorneys in the country and the most prolific writer on employment law in history. Richard challenged my partner Brian Murphy and me to help him write and edit a book, in less than three weeks, for attorneys and HR professionals on the myriad legal issues related to the pandemic. From that experience of working 16-hour days for three weeks straight with Richard and Brian, along with several other talented Sheppard Mullin attorneys as well as Jane Elliot from Castle Publications, we put together the *Employer's Guide to COVID-19 and Emerging Workplace Issues* (ISBN: 9781522198772). Working with Richard and Brian has been especially rewarding, and I look forward to collaborating on future projects with both of them in the years to come.

I also wish to express my appreciation for the support I have received from the leaders of Sheppard Mullin's Labor and Employment Practice Group—Kelly Hensley, Jonathan Stoller, and Greg Labate. I am also grateful to Matt Sonne for providing an extra set of eyes on the manuscript. I also wish to thank the firm's tremendous support staff that have assisted and guided me during this project, including Vickie Spang, Cindy Vargas, John Buchanan, and Rosa Vernetti.

To my publisher at SHRM, Matthew Davis, my editor, Montrese Hamilton, and their amazing team. I knew from our first conversation that SHRM was the right "home" for this book. Your support, encouragement, and guidance throughout this process has been first-rate. I look forward to continuing to work with you and the other professionals and members of SHRM to develop world-class training programs for HR professionals and leaders.

Special thanks to Donna Bedford, a professional coach extraordinaire. I credit Donna for helping me transform this book from an idea into a reality.

I clearly needed someone to gently push me in the right direction. Thanks for the push. And to bestselling author, HR guru, and all-around amazing guy, Paul Falcone. Words are truly inadequate for the appreciation I have for your guidance and advice. The feedback and encouragement you offered after reading the first few chapters gave me the confidence to continue with this project. Where other authors in this space may have seen me as a competitor, you, being such a stand-up person, welcomed me with open arms to the author club. I am also grateful for the feedback given to me by my friend, and leader in the MeToo Movement, Nicole Nevarez.

To my dear clients. The idea for this book came out of many conversations with my clients' senior executives, in-house counsel, HR professionals, and managers about the need for cogent and practical employment law training for frontline managers. My hope is that I lived up to your expectations and wrote a book that your organization's leaders will internalize and enjoy for many years to come. I appreciate every opportunity to serve as your attorney and work with you on solving complicated employment law issues. You are the reason I love being an attorney.

And finally, to my extended family and friends, your support is invaluable. To my parents, Allan and Wendy, thank you for instilling in me a love for writing and the gift of gab. To my brother, Jeremy, and sister, Lindsey, I am blessed to have you in my corner. To my second set of parents, my in-laws Brian and Merle, I am forever grateful for your support and friendship. And to Gwen, Paul, Julie, Stacey, and Aaron, and my ten nieces and nephews, thanks for keeping things lively and for your unconditional love and support. Lastly, to my friends and professional colleagues, I am grateful to be able to walk among you.

...

Endnotes

CHAPTER 2

1. Drew Desilver, "Job Categories Where Union Membership Has Fallen Off Most," *Pew Research Center,* April 27, 2015, https://www.pewresearch.org/fact-tank/2015/04/27/union-membership/?amp=1

2. Rakesh Kochhar, "Three-in-Ten U.S. Jobs Are Held by the Self-Employed and the Workers They Hire: Hiring More Prevalent Among Self-Employed Asians, Whites and Men," *Pew Research Center,* October 22, 2015, http://www.pewsocialtrends.org/2015/10/22/three-in-ten-us-jobs-are-held-by-the-self-employed-and-the-workers-they-hire/

CHAPTER 3

1. Sample EEO Statement: "The Company provides equal employment opportunities to all employees and applicants for employment and strongly prohibits discrimination and harassment of any type with respect to an individual's race, color, religion, age, sex, national origin, disability status, genetics, sexual orientation, gender identity or expression, protected veteran status, or any other characteristic protected by federal, state, or local laws."

2. Tanya Mulvey, "SHRM Survey Findings: Using Social Media for Talent Acquisition—Recruitment and Screening," *Society for Human Resource Management,* January 7, 2016, https://www.shrm.org/hr-today/trends-and-forecasting/research-and-surveys/Documents/SHRM-Social-Media-Recruiting-Screening-2015.pdf

CHAPTER 4

1. U.S. Census Bureau, *Current Population Survey, Annual Social and Economic (ASEC) Supplement: Table PINC-05: Work Experience in 2017—People 15 Years Old and Over by Total Money Earnings in 2017, Age, Race, Hispanic Origin, Sex, and Disability Status,* Accessed March 20, 2019, https://www.census.gov/data/tables/time-series/demo/income-poverty/cps-pinc/pinc-05.html

2. U.S. Census Bureau, *Current Population Survey, Annual Social and Economic (ASEC) Supplement: Table PINC-01. Selected Characteristics of People 15 Years and Over, by Total Money Income in 2017, Work Experience in 2017, Race, Hispanic Origin, and Sex,* Accessed March 20, 2019, https://www.census.gov/data/tables/time-series/demo/income-poverty/cps-pinc/pinc-01.html (unpublished calculation based on the mean annual pay for all women and men who worked full time, year-round in 2017, multiplied by the total number of women working full time, year-round in 2017).

3. Henry Holzer, Steven Raphael, and Michael A. Stoll, "Perceived Criminality, Criminal Background Checks, and the Racial Hiring Practices of Employers," *Journal of Law and Economics* 49, no. 2 (October 2006): 451–480.

CHAPTER 5

1. Emma E. Levine and Maurice E. Schweitzer, "The Affective and Interpersonal Consequences of Obesity," *Organizational Behavior and Human Decision Processes* 127 (March 2015): 66–84.

2. Paul A. Schulte et al., "Work, Obesity, and Occupational Safety and Health," *American Journal of Public Health* 97, no. 3 (March 1, 2007): 428–436.

3. Lynn K. Bartels and Cynthia R. Nordstrom, "Too Big to Hire: Factors Impacting Weight Discrimination," *Management Research Review* 36, no. 9 (August 2013): 868–881.

4. Alexander Green et al., "Implicit Bias among Physicians and its Prediction of Thrombolysis Decisions for Black and White Patients," *Journal of General Internal Medicine* 22, no. 9 (September 2007): 1231–1238.

5. Irene V. Blair, Jennifer E. Ma, and Alison P. Lenton, "Imagining Stereotypes Away: The Moderation of Implicit Stereotypes Through Mental Imagery," *Journal of Personality and Social Psychology* 81, no. 5 (November 2001): 828–841. See also Nilanjana Dasgupta and Anthony N. Greenwald, "On the Malleability of Automatic Attitudes: Combating Automatic Prejudice with Images of Admired and Disliked Individuals," *Journal of Personality and Social Psychology* 81, no. 5 (November 2001): 800–814. See also Thomas F. Pettigrew and Linda R. Tropp, "A Meta-Analytic Test of Intergroup Contact Theory," *Journal of Personality and Social Psychology* 90, no. 5 (May 2006): 751–783.

CHAPTER 7

1. Robert Sutton and Ben Wigert, "More Harm Than Good: The Truth About Performance Reviews," *Gallup Workplace,* May 6, 2019, https://www.gallup.com/workplace/249332/harm-good-truth-performance-reviews.aspx

2. Jack Zenger and Joseph Folkman, "Your Employees Want the Negative Feedback You Hate to Give," *Harvard Business Review,* January 15, 2014, https://hbr.org/2014/01/your-employees-want-the-negative-feedback-you-hate-to-give

3. See, e.g., *Hutson v. McDonnell Douglas Corp.,* 63 F.3d 771, 780 (8th Cir. 1995). ("The presence of subjectivity in employee evaluations is itself not a grounds for challenging those evaluations as discriminatory."); *Tomasso v. Boeing Co.,* 445 F.3d 702, 712 (3d Cir. 2006) ("It is the manager's perception of the employee's performance that is relevant.").

CHAPTER 10

1. *Hawn v. Exec. Jet Mgmt., Inc.,* 615 F.3d 1151, 1156 (9th Cir. 2010); *Godwin v. Hunt Wesson, Inc.,* 150 F.3d 1217, 1220 (9th Cir. 1998) (citing *McDonnell Douglas,* 411 U.S. at 802, 93 S.Ct. 1817).

2. *Hawn,* 615 F.3d at 1155.

3. *Wills v. Superior Court,* 195 Cal.App.4th 143, 170–171 (2011).

4. *Wills,* 195 Cal.App.4th at 143, 170–171.

CHAPTER 11

1. *Brennan v. Townsend & O'Leary Enterprises, Inc.,* 199 Cal.App.4th 1336, 1347–1348 (2011).

About the Author

Adam Rosenthal is a Labor and Employment partner in the law firm of Sheppard, Mullin, Richter & Hampton LLP in the firm's Del Mar (San Diego) and Los Angeles offices. In addition to advising clients on employment law issues and representing employers before federal and state courts, and in arbitration proceedings throughout the country, Adam lectures extensively to in-house attorneys, HR professionals, and managers on a variety of employment law topics. Adam has received numerous recognitions and awards, including an AV Peer Review Rating from Martindale-Hubbell, as well as the BTI Client Service All Star award.

Adam received his law degree from the University of California, Davis, and his undergraduate degree in history from the University of California, Los Angeles. Prior to law school, Adam taught middle school English and history in Oakland, California, as part of the *Teach For America* program. While in law school, Adam represented over 250,000 University of California students as the student member of the Board of Regents. Adam is actively involved in civil rights issues and serves as the chair of the Anti-Defamation League's San Diego region. Adam lives in San Diego, California, with his wife and three children.

Index